*For my father who taught me simplicity and
my mother who taught me tenacity*
　　　　　　　　—Spike Carlsen

*For my late brother Ken and
my loving wife Deb*
　　　　　　　　—Bill Zuehlke

Contents

Chapter 3: Kitchen and Dining Room

Chapter 4: Outdoors

Introduction

One of my favorite pieces of furniture is a side table built by my Uncle Bob over 40 years ago. It's no more than four 1x3s connected to a pair of plywood discs, but it's endured a dozen moves, the burden of a few thousand magazines, even a cigarette burn from my reckless brother-in-law, Ray. It's not fancy (the good part of this, I guess, is that it's never gone out of style), but it is solid, well designed and easy to build—like the projects in this book. In fact, it inspired one of the first projects in this book.

Sure you can buy a screw-together table from a Big Box store for $19.99—but in the end, you wind up with a screw-together table from a Big Box store. There's no chance to tweak dimensions, shape, style or wood. And do you REALLY feel a sense of accomplishment when you toss your screwdriver back in the junk drawer when you're done screwing it together?

Ridiculously Simple Furniture Projects provides you with plans and instructions for building, well, just what the title says. It also provides you with something harder to come by these days—the feeling of satisfaction in having built something with your own two hands; something you can point to and tell your grandkids "I built that 40 years ago." And you'll save money to boot.

We've also scattered information on safety, tools and skills throughout the book. We didn't lump it all at the beginning because you want to build furniture, not read about it. But if you're looking for more details on a certain technique or tool, check the index and Table of Contents; there's a good chance you'll find the information you need.

Before building any piece of furniture in this book (in fact, before building *anything*) we encourage you to "grok" the project first. And just what does *that* mean? In Robert Heinlein's science fiction novel, *Stranger in a Strange Land*, he coined the word "grok" to explain the notion of understanding someone or something "so thoroughly that the observer becomes part of the observed—to merge, blend, intermarry" ... well, let's not get too touchy-feely here. But you get the idea, right? Before rolling up your sleeves, you should have the big picture. You should grok what you're about to build, how it goes together and in what order.

And here's why: This is YOUR furniture, not ours. You know what color, size and style you like, so embellish, improvise, scale down and scale up as you see fit. For most projects we include illustrations, dimensions, even life-size templates, but our hope is you'll use this information as a starting point and inspiration for building what you like and need.

There are a few projects that aren't really and truly *ridiculously simple*—maybe *pretty simple* would be a better label. But we included them because, after you've gained confidence building some of the easier projects, our guess is you'll be itching to tackle something a little more difficult.

So whether you're a woodworker who likes to dabble, a homeowner or apartment dweller looking to furnish a few rooms or a complete rookie that's been tempted to give woodworking a shot, this book's for you. Roll up your sleeves. Enjoy.

Spike Carlson

Uncle Bob's Craftsman Side Table

Two store-bought discs, a few 1x3s—and you're a Craftsman

My Uncle Bob was one of those classic uncles that would pull nickels out of your ear and tickle you until milk came out your nose. He worked most of his life as a butcher—and I suspect his daily use of a band saw for cutting pork chops naturally inclined him to use the same tool for crafting furniture. This piece was inspired by a table Uncle Bob made 40 years ago; one that still serves as a side table next to my reading chair in the den.

STUFF YOU'LL NEED

15-in. precut disc	1
18-in. precut disc	1
1" x 3" x 8' pine	2

How to build it

You don't need a band saw to create this table. The round top and round lower shelf are precut discs you can purchase at a home center. Glue and screw the leg braces to the large top disc (photo 1) so the 5-degree cuts on the ends are angling outward. Cut ¾" x 2½" notches in the lower disc spaced equally around the perimeter (photo 2).

Cut the legs to length, with 5-degree angles on each end, and create the decorative cutouts as shown in photo 3. Use a backer board so the bit doesn't splinter the wood as it emerges through the backside of the board. You can cut the slot "freehand" or use a straight-cutting jig (shown on page 27) to help guide your jigsaw.

The trim head screws used to secure the discs to the legs (photos 3 and 4) are simply drywall screws with a thinner shank and smaller head. Predrill the holes to minimize the chance of splitting the wood.

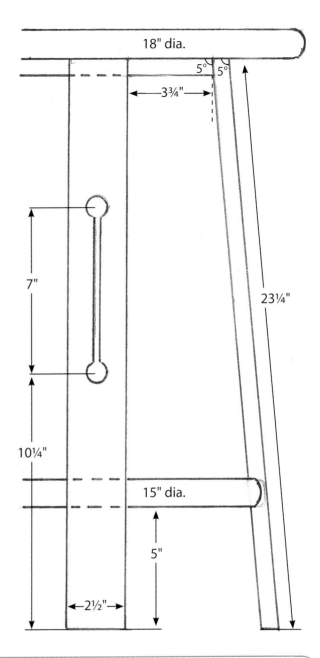

Wood Screws vs. Drywall Screws

Though you'll find thousands of screws at your hardware store, in the end they all do one thing: Clamp two things together. They do this by using threads to pull themselves into the "bottom" piece, while the head clamps a "top" piece against it.

Wood screws have a straight section near the head and a threaded section near the tip, while **drywall screws** are threaded along their entire length (always use coarse, rather than fine threaded screws.) Whichever type you use, make sure the two pieces being joined are positioned tightly against one another so the glue can do its job and the threads don't actually hold the two pieces away from one another. Drilling a larger pilot hole in the top piece allows the threads to pull the pieces together more easily.

1 Glue and nail braces in an "X" shape on the bottom of the tabletop. Note the ends of the braces are angled outward at 5-degrees.

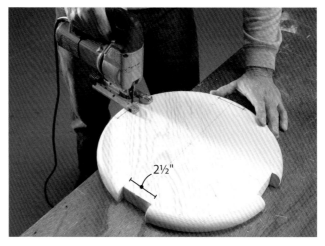

2 Divide the smaller disc into 4 equal pie slices, then measure and mark out the notches for the 1x3 legs. Cut the notches with a jigsaw.

3 Drill holes in the legs to create the ends of the decorative cutouts. Cut out the slot with a jigsaw guided by a "straight cutting jig," similar to the one used with the circular saw shown in this book.

TIP ★ *Easier Driving*

Lots of the projects in this book—including this one—use "drywall" or "all purpose" screws to hold things together. To make them easier to drive in (and quieter), run the threads across a wax candle to lubricate them.

4 Secure the tops of the legs to the large disc using glue and trim head drywall screws. Prop the bottom disc on scrap 2x4s and position the legs in the slots. Make sure the upper and lower disc align and that the table isn't leaning to one side, then glue and screw the legs to the bottom disc.

Tic-Tac-Toe Shelf

A unique shelf made from four (almost) identical boards

Ginger, the tic tac toe playing chicken that works at the Tropicana Casino in Vegas (true story), wins or draws over 99% of the games she plays. This shelf, named after Ginger's favorite game, is so easy to build she might be able to tackle this project, too.

This shelf consists of four boards that are all the same size and shape. Hung on the wall it provides six compartments, good for stowing iPod docking stations, speakers, books or your paperweight collection. You can even put hooks in the three lower compartments and use them for hanging keys, jewelry or glasses. Best of all, you can build it for, well, chicken feed.

STUFF
YOU'LL NEED
1" x 6" x 8'   1

How to build it

We used oak for our shelves, but you can use pine, maple or any other wood. Cut the 1x6 into four 24 inch long pieces. Tape together a "board sandwich" (photo 1) and mark the slots across all four of them based on the measurements shown in the illustration.

Be as accurate as possible when cutting the notches; if they're too narrow the shelves won't fit together and if they're too wide, there will be gaps where they intersect. Use a handsaw or jig saw to extend the cuts so they're 2-¾ inches deep, then use a sharp ¾-in. chisel (photo 2) to remove the bottoms of the notches.

Draw the 18-in. arc on one board using a screw as a center point and tape measure as a giant compass (see illustration). Cut the curve (photo 3), then use that board as a template for marking the other three. Notice that two of the curves are on the notched sides and two are made on the un-notched sides. (Don't forget this or you'll have one funny looking shelf.) Use sandpaper and a sanding block—or power sander if you own one—to smooth the curves and slightly soften the edges of the boards (photo 4). Stain and apply finish to the boards if you wish.

Interlock the boards. Hang it using sawtooth-type picture hanger brackets installed near each end of the top horizontal shelf.

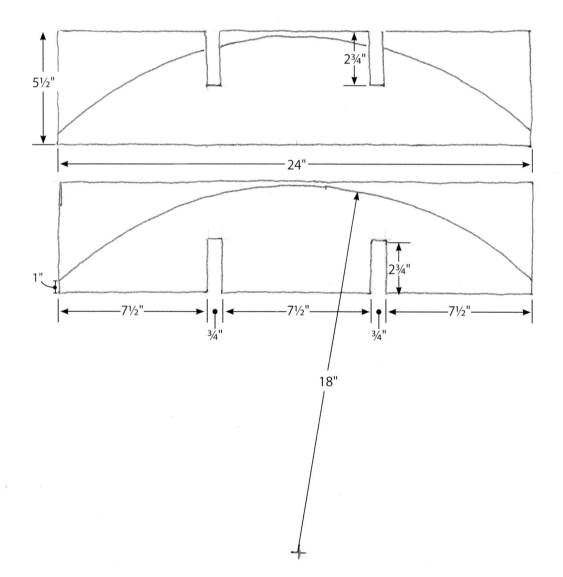

1 Cut the 1x6s to length, then tape or clamp them together. Mark the positions of the two slots across all four boards, then use a circular saw set to its deepest cutting depth to cut the sides of the notches.

2 Separate the boards, then use a jigsaw or handsaw to finish cutting the notches to their proper depth. Use a sharp chisel to cleanly chop out the bottom of the notch.

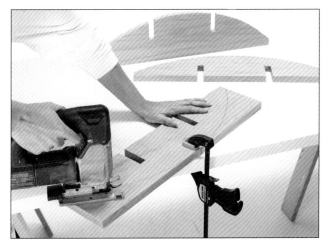

3 Draw the 18-in. radius arc on one board (see the illustration) and cut it out. Use that board as a template for marking the other three boards.

4 Clamp the four boards together then use a sanding block or power sander to smooth the curved surfaces and soften the edges.

A Few Tidbits About Oak

It seems like everywhere we turn we encounter something made of oak: Oak cabinets, flooring, tables, chairs, window trim and closet doors. Even cork flooring and the cork we pop from our wine bottles come from the cork oak tree. We love oak—but that's nothing new. The Druids used to worship oaks. In ancient Europe, oak trees were so revered that anyone caught vandalizing one had their navel nailed to the tree and was forced to walk around it until they were—well—inside out. One doesn't know how much of that is urban legend or Medieval trash talk, but the fact is, people love oak.

There are over 200 species of the tree. Though important today, it was indispensable in the past. It was the wood of choice for shipbuilding and for making the charcoal that stoked mankind's earliest industrial efforts—making iron, glass and brick. The durable wood was used to make gears and other parts of clocks, windmills, water wheels and other machines. The bark was used for tanning leather and oak galls were used to make the earliest forms of ink (that's what Leonardo used). Oak barrels were used to transport nearly everything. There were even some Native American cultures that subsisted on acorns.

Oak could arguably be christened the most important wood in history.

Working (Towards Being) Accident Free

Don't you hate it when you buy a toaster and the instruction manual has 15 pages of safety warnings and only one page of actual instructions. You get warnings like: DO NOT OPERATE TOASTER WHILE IN BATHTUB and DO NOT USE APPLIANCE TO IRON CLOTHES OR DEFROST REFRIGERATOR. Yet, when it comes to the thing you really want to know—how to get the crumbs out of the bottom—they don't tell you how.

Well, this book isn't like that. We're going to give you two pages of warnings and 120 pages of useful instructions. We're going to presume you have common sense—because common sense can prevent most accidents.

Spike's theory of accident-ivity

When you walk through the woods and a branch suddenly snaps off and bonks you in the head, that's an accident. There's nothing you could have done—short of staying in bed that day—that would have prevented it from happening. When you walk through your workshop or basement and a pipe clamp falls off the workbench and breaks your toe, that's not an accident—because it's something you had control over preventing.

There are three things in the workshop that can cause accidents: Tools, wood and people (and combinations thereof). In every case, there are things you can do to reduce the chances of a "true accident" down to almost zero. Let's take a quick look at each.

The wood. One frequent accident has to do with "binding," which happens when the cut or "kerf" you're making with a circular saw or table saw pinches or binds the blade. If wood is wet or under tension, that kerf can close up and pinch the blade—and something's gotta give. If you see that beginning to happen, drive a tapered shim into the kerf to keep it from closing up.

There are other kinds of binding. If you're cutting a board with each end of that board sitting on a sawhorse, the kerf is going to close up and pinch the blade. The saw may zing back toward you or the board may launch away from you—but something is going to happen. Always make sure gravity is on your side and scrap pieces can "fall away."

Keep fingers out of the projected path of utility knives and other sharp tools in case something slips.

Clamp down work pieces, especially when you're boring holes in them with large drill bits. This board, unclamped, could become a whirling helicopter blade, hitting you in places where you really don't want to get hit.

Also look out for flying knots. If the board you're cutting has a loose knot you may be cutting though, see if you can rotate it so the knot is out of the way. Always wear eye protection—even if it's prescription glasses with hardened lenses like I wear. And clamp things down, especially if your work piece is small and you're tempted to put your hands too close to the blade or bit.

The tool. In rare instances a tool, bit, belt or blade will break and cause an accident, but for the most part, tool accidents are "people" accidents. Always use sharp blades and bits; more accidents happen when forcing a tool with a dull blade or bit than any

Keep your hand a safe distance from the path of fasteners you're installing, particularly when driven with a nail gun.

Avoid binding the blade. Arrange your work piece so the scrap will fall away after the cut. Using an angle square to guide your saw will also help minimize binding.

other time. Another common accidents is the "oops I didn't know it was turned on" accident. This includes plugging in a belt sander that has the trigger locked in the ON position; that can damage the tool, the wood, your workbench and you.

Use all your senses when you work. A blade that's binding will sound and smell differently than a blade that's cutting smoothly.

The person. The cardinal rule that will avoid most accidents is to simply ask yourself the question, "What if?"—and then answer it correctly. What if this drill bit slips while my hand is right next to it? What if I accidentally hit the ON switch while I'm changing this jigsaw blade? What if this piece of wood I'm drilling starts spinning while my kid is standing there?

Needless to say (but I'm going to say it anyway) picking up sharp tools after a night of partying or arguing with your teenage daughter about the spider tattoo she just got on her forehead is not a good idea. Head to your workshop because you want to build something, not wreck something.

The combination. The chances of an accident greatly increases when all three factors—wood, tool and people—come into play. Let's look at two scenarios.

In scenario #1, Mr. Accident is cutting a board on a table saw. He's using a dull blade to cut wet wood and he's standing directly behind the part of the board that's between the blade and the saw fence. Mr. Accident is going to push the board harder so he's going to be off balance, the dull blade is going to work harder and heat up faster, the heat from the blade is going to make the kerf close faster. And when that board binds and shoots back, he's going to be in its flight path.

Wear hearing protectors while using power tools, compressors and shop vacuums. When my ear muffs aren't on my ears, I prop them up on my head so I always know where to find them. You may look like Mickey Mouse, but at least you'll be a mouse with good hearing.

TIP ★ *Be Prepared*

Carry a BandAid in your billfold. I've gone through dozens of them—both in the workshop and out in the real world.

In scenario #2, Mr. Tenfingers is using a sharp blade to cut dry wood and he's using a push stick so he can stand off to the side. He's reduced his chances of an accident to almost zero.

Triple-Tier Basket Stand

An amazingly versatile storage stand, made with an amazingly versatile tool

You've seen chests of drawers—well here's a "chest of baskets." It can be used in nearly any room—in the bathroom for storing towels, the entryway for organizing hats and gloves, the bedroom for workout clothes, even in the kitchen for veggies or hand towels.

We purchased our baskets at a Michael's craft store, but lots of other retailers like Pier 1, West Elm and Ikea also carry them. Make sure to buy your baskets first; you need to construct your chest based on their dimensions.

To keep the frame of the chest both lightweight and strong, we used biscuit joinery. It's a clever way of joining wood, and a technique you can use with many other projects. See the sidebar for more details on how to do it.

STUFF YOU'LL NEED

1" x 2"	32 li. ft.*
¾" square dowel	6 li. ft.
¾" cove molding	6 li. ft.
¾" x 13" x 13 ¾" plywood	1 pc.

li. ft. = lineal feet

How to build it

Layout all four legs at the same time to ensure the framework is uniform and square (photo 1). Keep picturing how your baskets will sit on the runners—especially if you're using baskets smaller or larger than ours; it will help you avoid mental errors. Cut the side crosspieces to length. Use the biscuit joiner to cut slots in the edges of the uprights and ends of the crosspieces (photo 2). Apply glue to the biscuits and slots (photo 3), insert the biscuits in both ends of all four crosspieces in each side, then clamp these "ladders" together and set them aside until the glue dries.

Install the front and back crosspieces that hold the side "ladders" together. The four back crosspieces are installed even with the four side crosspieces. The three front crosspieces that will support the baskets lie flat. Glue and nail these crosspieces in place, make sure the rack is square, then set it aside until the glue dries. Install the basket runners (photo 4) even with the flat crosspieces that run across the front.

Install the ¾-in. plywood top, then apply cove molding to cover the edges (photo 5).

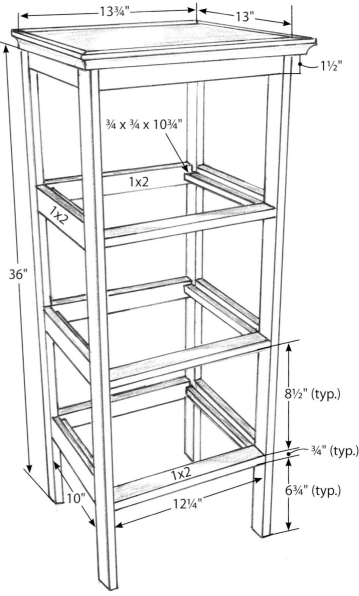

1 Make layout marks on the four legs by clamping them together and marking all four at the same time. The "X" in each set of lines indicates the center of the basket runners (and the center of your biscuit joint); the outer lines represent the edges of the 1x2 horizontal cross members.

2 Cut the grooves for the biscuits in the ends of the crosspieces and sides of the uprights. See the sidebar on the next page for more information.

3 Use glue and biscuits to secure the components that create the two side "ladders." Use clamps to hold the uprights and crosspieces together until the glue dries.

Side ladders

Runners

4 Install the front and back cross pieces that hold the two ladder sides together. The front crosspieces lie flat so the baskets can slide in and out. Add the ¾-in. x ¾-in. basket runners to the sides.

¾" Plywood top

5 Glue and nail the ¾-in. plywood top to the top of the frame, then apply cove molding to neaten up and disguise the edges.

The Biscuit Joiner—A Tasty Little Tool

Using a biscuit or plate joiner is a superb way of joining two pieces of wood in situations where it would be difficult (or ugly) to use nails or screws. The joint is strong, invisible and easy to create.

The system is similar to doweling, except slots are cut instead of holes and biscuits are used instead of dowels. The special compressed wood biscuits expand when they come in contact with moisture in the glue. When the biscuits are positioned in the adjoining slots of two pieces of wood, the glue and the expansion of the biscuit help lock the pieces together. Since the biscuits are placed in slots that are wider than the biscuit, you can adjust the joint a little after butting the two pieces together.

The basic procedure goes like this:

- Determine where you want to join the two boards, then make a center mark on both boards where you want the biscuit installed (as shown in the two photos).
- Position the center mark of the biscuit cutter on the center mark of the board, then push the handle toward the board until it stops. A small blade will emerge to cut a crescent-shaped slot.
- Apply glue to both sides of the biscuit and to the joint. Install the biscuit in one slot, then position the other board and push that into the biscuit. Clamp the boards together.

The slot is usually centered on the width of the board, but the height of the front plate can be adjusted so the slot can be cut anywhere. The joiner can also be adjusted to cut slots of varying depth to accommodate different-size biscuits. We only used the biscuit joiner to make simple butt joints, but they can be used to connect right-angle joints, mitered joints and other joints.

You can buy a good basic entry-level tool for under $100. Biscuits cost under a nickel apiece.

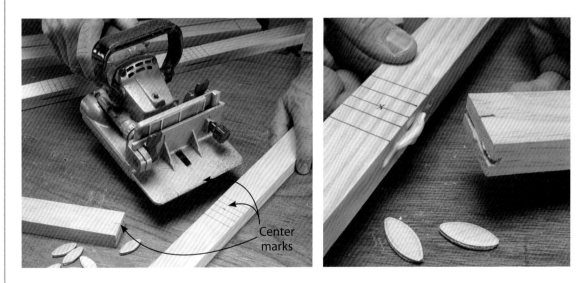

Center marks

World's Simplest Toy Chest
A ridiculously simple way to make an attractive toy chest or cabinet

One smart way to create "Ridiculously Simple" furniture is to take advantage of the ridiculously inexpensive building materials available. Sure, your persnickety woodworker brother-in-law may wince at the thought of using a store-bought cabinet as the starting point—but if you don't have the sophisticated tools required for cabinetmaking, this technique allows you to build that toy chest for your granddaughter anyway. And if you need a storage cabinet, all you have to do is make a few minor alterations and you can have that, too (see the sidebar.)

STUFF YOU'LL NEED

15" x 30" oak wall cabinet	1
⅜" x 4" oak bead board	30 li. Ft.
1" oak corner molding	18 li. Ft.

Lid support bracket(s), handle, bun feet (or screw-in curtain rod finials)

How to build it

Cut a ¾ in. piece of plywood to fit inside the cabinet and install it in the bottom (formerly the back) of the cabinet to reinforce it.

Glue and nail ⅜ in. tongue & groove bead board—often sold as wainscoting at your home center—to the sides of your cabinet (photo 1). You could also use ¼-in. oak plywood. Install 1" x 1" corner molding to frame and create a finished edge along the top and bottom of the cabinet edges (photo 2). The bun feet we used for the trunk (photo 3) are actually inexpensive curtain rod finials purchased for $2 apiece.

After staining and finishing the piece, install the handle and lid support. If little ones will be playing with it or near it, install a soft-closing or kid-safe lid support available at specialty woodworking stores like Rockler and Woodcraft.

> ### TIP ★ *Error-Free Measuring*
>
> Cutting L-shaped corner molding can be confusing because you're measuring to the inside of the "L". It's easiest to cut one end at 45-degrees, hold it in place, mark the other end, then make your cut.

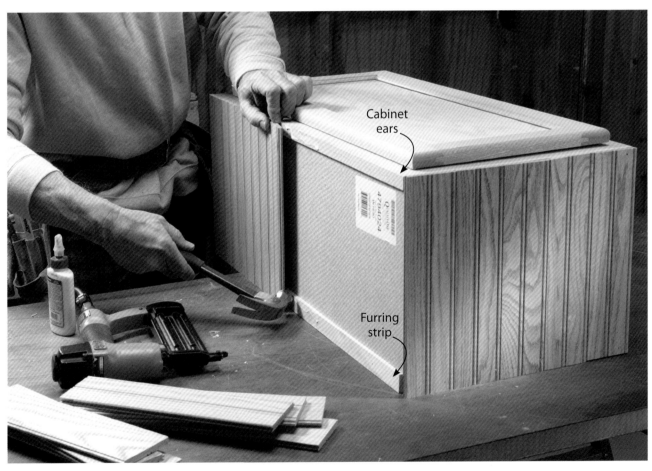

Cabinet ears

Furring strip

1 Fur out the sides of the chest with thin strips of wood the same thickness as the "ears" on the cabinet face front. Glue and nail the bead board in place.

Curtain rod finials

2 Install the L-shaped corner molding along the top and bottom edges.

3 Pre-drill holes and install the feet. We used inexpensive curtain rod finials purchased in packs of two.

... And If You Need A Storage Cabinet

Use the same basic steps for building this legged cabinet as you would for building the toy chest. The main difference is you'll install the feet on a different side. You may want to install plywood for the cabinet "top" so you have a smooth, rather than bumpy, surface for setting things on. If so, apply moldings to the edges of the plywood to cover the raw edges.

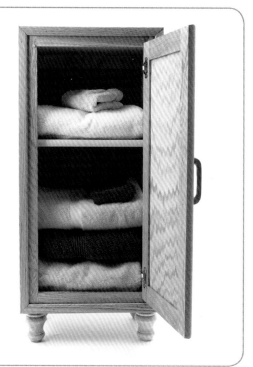

The feet shown are an off-the-shelf variety found at Lowe's home center. For an even wider variety of options, check out the Adams Wood Products website at www.adamswoodproducts.com. They have feet in every size, shape and species imaginable. Some feet require the installation of inexpensive "hanger bolt" brackets; check what kind of threads the legs' mounting bolts have and install them if necessary.

TIP ★ *Tighter Looking Miters*

A sneaky way to make sure mitered corners look great is to apply glue to both pieces, nail them in place, then use fine sandpaper to sand the joint while it's still wet. The glue will combine with the fine sanding dust to fill any small gaps.

Frank Lloyd Wrong Chair & Ottoman

Frankie loved using plywood for furniture. Now it's your turn.

There *has* to be an easy chair in a book titled *Ridiculously Simple Furniture Projects*, right? Well, wc soon discovered, most easy chairs aren't really all that easy to design or build. Upholstery, springs, weird joints—oof dah. So we scratched our heads, borrowed a few ideas from the great Frank Lloyd Wright—where the chair got its name—and came up with this design. This chair can be made from a 2' x 8' sheet of ¾-in plywood and doesn't require much in the way of tricky joinery, fancy tools or exotic upholstering skills. It's sturdy and lightweight. Best of all, it's comfortable. If you build the optional ottoman, it's even more comfortable.

STUFF YOU'LL NEED

For the chair:

¾" x 2' x 8' solid core plywood	1
1" x 3" x 8' clear pine	1
1" x 2" x 4' clear pine	1

Chair cushion material:

½" x 2' x 4' plywood	1
2" foam	6 sq. ft.
Upholstery cloth	8 sq. ft.

Frank Lloyd Wright

Though best known for his architecture, Frank Lloyd Wright was also a gifted and prolific furniture designer. He often designed the furnishings for the houses he built, right down to the upholstery and carpet. Rumor has it, he was once even tempted to design an occupant's clothes. He experimented with lots of different materials including precast concrete, pyrex tubing and—what for its day was a new-fangled material—plywood.

Image from www.architonic.com

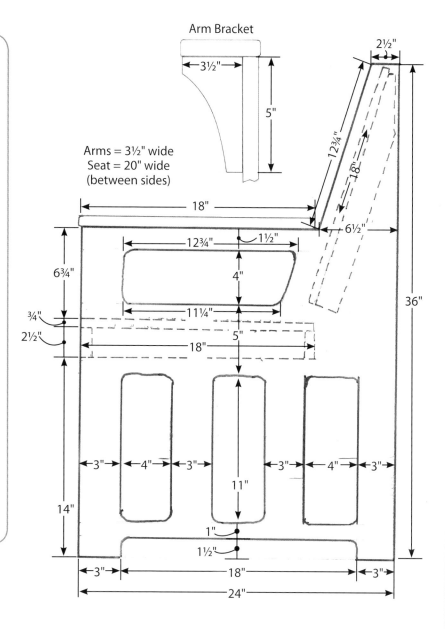

Arm Bracket

3½"
5"
2½"

Arms = 3½" wide
Seat = 20" wide
(between sides)

12¾"
18"
6½"
36"

18"
6¾"
¾"
2½"
12¾"
1½"
4"
11¼"
5"
18"

3" 4" 3" 11" 3" 4" 3"
1"
1½"
14"

3" 18" 3"
24"

The Footstool

Building the footstool uses the same materials and techniques as the chair. If you build it four inches shorter than we show, you can store it under the chair.

STUFF YOU'LL NEED

For the footstool:

¾" x 2' x 4' solid core plywood	1
1" x 3" x 6' clear pine	1
1" x 2" x 2' clear pine	1
Footstool cushion material:	
½" x 2' x 2' plywood	1
2" foam	3 sq. ft.
Upholstery cloth	4 sq. ft.

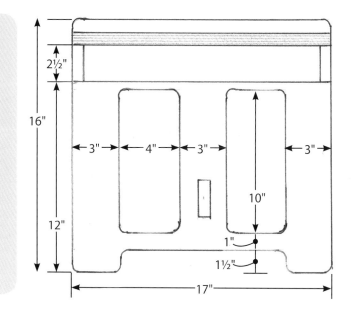

2½"
16"
3" 4" 3" 3"
10"
12"
1"
1½"
17"

How to build it

Start by transferring the measurements and layout lines from the illustration onto your plywood (photo 1). It's easiest to layout one side of the chair, cut it out, then use that as a template for drawing the other side— that way the two sides will be symmetrical. But if you prefer drawing each side individually, that's fine, too. It's your time.

There are 18 radius corners for the cutouts in each side of the chair; the fastest, most accurate way to make them is to use a hole saw. To establish the center of each hole use a spacer block to make intersecting marks ¾ of an inch away from each cutout edge (photo 2). Drill from both sides as explained in photo 3, to minimize splintering the wood. Finish cutting out the rectangles using a circular saw and jigsaw. Round over the edges of both faces of the side panels using a router and round over bit (photo 4).

Secure the 1x3 seat frame and the 1x2 back cleat to one side panel (photo 5), then attach the other side. Secure the plywood seat to the seat frame using glue and drywall screws, then secure the plywood back to the back cleats (photo 6) the same way.

Cut ½-in. plywood to create bases for the seat and back cushions. The base and foam for the seat cushion should be ½ inch smaller in both directions than the actual seat. The base (and foam) for the back cushion should be ½ inch narrower and five or six inches shorter than the actual back. Lay your upholstery face-down on a clean work surface, then lay the foam and plywood on top. Wrap the cloth snuggly around the plywood (photo 7), then staple it in place. Make sure to stretch the fabric uniformly and fold the corners neatly for the best appearance. Use drywall screws to secure the cushions in place (photo 8).

Build the ottoman using the same basic materials and steps. If you build the ottoman 4 inches shorter than the measurements in the illustration, it will tuck neatly under the chair (wish we'd thought of that sooner!).

1 Transfer the measurements from the illustration to the plywood. Use a drywall square to speed the process and increase accuracy.

2 Use a ¾-in.-wide strip of wood to mark the centers for the 1½" hole saw bit you'll use to "cut out" the inside corners of the cutouts. There are 18 holes needed for each side, so use a sharp bit.

3 Drill through the plywood until the pilot bit pokes through the other side. Flip the plywood over, insert the pilot bit in the hole and finish boring the hole. Use a jigsaw to cut out the remaining part of the rectangles.

4 Use a router with a ¼-in. round over bit to round the edges on both sides of the plywood. Use 180-grit sandpaper to smooth and blend rough edges or uneven spots.

5 Build the four-sided 1x3 frame that will support the plywood seat, then secure it to one of the plywood sides. Add the 1x2 cleat that supports the plywood back of the chair. Secure the other plywood side to the frame.

Back cleat

6 Use glue and 1-¼-in. drywall screws to secure the ¾ in. plywood seat and plywood back to their supports.

7 Cut a piece of plywood and a piece of upholstery foam ½-in. smaller than the seat. Position them upside-down over the cloth, wrap the cloth around the edges, apply a little tension, then staple it to the plywood.

½"
plywood

2" foam

Picking Upholstery

I walked into JoAnn Fabrics to select upholstery for the chair and was knocked silly by the selection available. There was over 20 kinds of blue denim alone; faded denim, bright blue denim, "mom jeans" denim, you name it. The fabric I selected wasn't actual upholstery material, but I liked the look and feel of it. The salesperson told me it wouldn't last as long as the real thing, but it was tough enough to last for years.

The store also sold foam in a variety of thicknesses and densities. I went with a medium-density, 2-in. thick foam.

8 Use a few drywall screws to secure the padded seat and back to the chair. Note that the arms and arm supports have been added. If you're going to apply a finish, do it before installing the cushions.

Whimsical Wall Shelf
Use $8 crown molding blocks—and the hard part is done

This wall shelf may look like it required a lot of fancy tools and head scratching, but it didn't. The bottom brackets are pre-built "corbel" blocks, normally used for installing crown molding, that you can buy at home centers or online for a few bucks. This is a project where you can really put your creative juices to work. There are hundreds of different types of moldings available—which means there are hundreds of different types of shelves you can build.

Stuff You'll Need

Two EverTrue 5½" pine "mid-crown corners" or corbels (about $8/each from Lowes) or something similar.

¾" cove molding

1x4 and 1x6 lumber

Make it your own

Use this project as inspiration for creating your own unique shelves.

- Don't limit yourself to the moldings shown here; there are dozens of different ones available at your local lumberyard or home center.
- Make your shelves as long or as short as you wish (though shelves longer than 5 ft. might sag).
- Use a single corbel to create a short mini-shelf for displaying collectibles, art, photos or knick knacks.
- If you're short on wall space, position the corbels far enough apart so you can install the shelf over a window. With a little extra creativity, you can even turn this into a combination shelf/valance.

How to build it

Cut the 1x4 and 1x6 to length, then cut, glue and nail cove molding along three edges of each board. Cut and install cove molding on three sides of the crown molding blocks, too (photo 1). Glue and nail the narrower shelf to the wider one, then nail the corbels to the narrow shelf (photo 2). Stain or paint the shelf (we used spray paint), install two sawtooth-type picture-hanging brackets, then hang the shelf on the wall.

1 Cut and install cove molding to surround three sides of both boards and both corbels. It's faster and more accurate to mark the moldings in place than measuring.

2 Glue and nail all the components to one another. Predrill the holes so the molding does not split. A needle-nose pliers works better than fingers for holding brads and small nails.

To Hammer or to Shoot?

You may have looked at the pneumatic finish nailer used in many of these projects and thought, "Ooh that looks expensive—or tricky to use—or scary—or all three." But you'd be wrong on all three counts. They're actually relatively inexpensive, simple to operate and safe. On a recent trip to Home Despot we found a finish nailer, compressor and hose for $80; more than the cost of a hammer but, when you consider the benefits, worth every penny.

For starters, a finish nailer allows you to hold the pieces together with one hand, then join them with the pull of a trigger. It allows you to work faster and more accurately. The nailer sets the nail to the right depth so you don't need to go back and sink the head with a nail set. And you eliminate the possibility of wrecking your projects with the dreaded hammerhead "pecker mark."

And they're safe. Sure, you read the occasional story in the *National Enquirer* about the guy who accidentally nails both feet to the floor with a nail gun and has to wait until his coworkers get back from lunch to get free—but that's with a really big gun, shooting really big nails, operated by a really big idiot. Just keep the hand holding the pieces together well out of the projected path of the nail, make sure the nose of the nailer is steady and in the right position before pulling the trigger, and wear protective goggles and hearing protectors.

Another huge bonus is, you wind up with an air compressor that can do lots of other things—like blow up bike and car tires, inflate air mattresses, and blow sawdust off of your workbench and you.

In this and other projects in the book we show a hammer and nails being used—and that's a legitimate path to travel if you're not ready to take the trip to Pneumatic-ville. Lots of people enjoy the peace and quiet of working only with hand tools. But to be honest with you, when the camera's not rolling, we grab the pneumatic nailer and pop things together to get ready for the next photo as quickly as possible.

Bifold Coffee Table

The world's cheapest, lightest, easiest-to-make table

Hollow-core bifold doors are cheap, easy to cut, and lightweight—which makes them the perfect candidate for the world's cheapest, easiest, lightest coffee table. The basic table consists of a 12-to-18-inch-wide hollow core bifold door, a few strips of wood and some shelf brackets. You can embellish and modify this basic frame as explained in "Make It Your Own."

STUFF YOU'LL NEED

Bifold door (12 to 18 in. wide)	1
1" x 2" x 6'	1
¼" x 2" x 10' pine	1
Brackets	4 or 8

Note: We installed Milano Shelf Brackets (#0087), $3.50 each, from John Sterling Corporation (www. johnsterling.com); available at most home centers and hardware stores.

How to build it

Cut 12- to 16-in.-long legs from each end of the door. You can minimize splintering the thin veneer by doing three things: 1) Cut the door with the good face down, 2) Use a fine-tooth blade in your circular saw, 3) Mark your cut line with a utility knife (photo 1), then run your saw blade just to the outside of the line; one side of the cut will splinter, but the other will be crisp.

Cut four filler strips the thickness of the door's core—they'll be about 1-⅛ in. wide. Use two strips to fill in the open ends of the table top (photo 2) and two for the leg cleats (photo 3.) Use glue and finish nails to secure the filler blocks and cleats in place. Once the glue has set, install the legs as shown in photo 3. Add the four brackets (photo 4) to brace the legs; we used shelf brackets. Install brackets on both sides of the legs for even greater stability. Secure them to the outer edges where the screws have solid wood to bite into.

Install cork tiles to cover the top, then add the edge trim to cover the edges of the door and the surface material. If you think people will be sitting (or dancing) on the table, cover the surface with something solid and durable like laminate flooring.

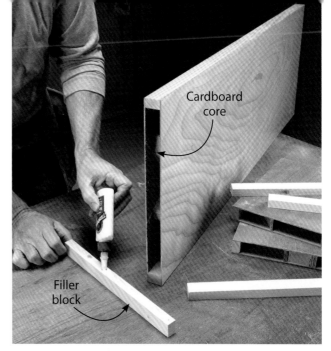

1 Cut the 12" to 16" long legs from each end of the door. Cut "good face down" and mark your line by scoring with a utility knife to minimize splintering. Cut the tabletop to length (or leave it that length).

2 Cut filler blocks and cleats to fit into the hollow ends, then glue and nail them in place. You may need to use a block of wood to tap the cardboard core further into the door.

3 Apply glue to the leg cleats, slide the legs over them, then nail them in place. Use a square to make sure the legs are square to the top.

4 Install brackets to secure the legs to the top and prevent them from wiggling or collapsing. Add them to both sides of the legs for extra rigidity. Add trim and a more durable top surface.

Make it your own

Once you've created the basic table, there are three areas where you can customize it to your liking.

- **Leg brackets.** We used inexpensive shelf brackets from a local home center. You can use plain or fancy ones made of wood or metal.

- **Trim material.** We used ¼" x 2" boards to create the border around the top. We let it extend ¼" above the top to cover the edges of the cork we added. You can use any dimension or style molding you want—or leave the edges plain and simply paint them.

- **Top material.** We glued 12" x 12" cork squares to the top to create a more durable surface. You can use pre-finished flooring, tile or other material.

Oak Hallway Mirror
Build this with the fairest tool of all—the pocket screw jig!

When I saw a mirror similar to this at a furniture store with a $195 price tag on it I said to myself, "Self, I bet you could build something like that for a fourth the price. And do a better job. And make it the exact size you need."

This project takes wood, moldings, pegs and a plain old mirror you can buy at any home center, and combines them into a functional, attractive hallway looking glass. This project also introduces you to the pocket screw jig—an ingenious fastening system you can use for all sorts of other projects in this book and elsewhere.

Stuff You'll Need
1" x 3" and 1" x 6" oak
Crown molding
Oak Shaker pegs
Mirror

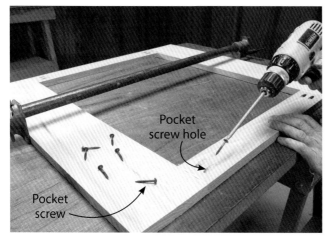

1 Cut the four frame members to length, then connect them using pocket screws (see sidebar). Make certain the boards are lying flat and the surfaces are flush to one another.

2 Install the crown molding. It's easy to break the little side returns if you nail them in place, so simply apply glue to the ends and hold them in place with tape until the glue dries.

3 Bore holes for the pegs, apply glue to the pegs, then insert and twist them into the holes. Also glue and nail the ¼ in. backer plywood in place.

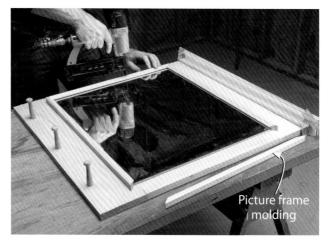

4 Cut the picture frame molding to length, then glue and nail it in place. Think twice before cutting the pieces; you need to mark the molding based on where the mirror hits the groove in the back of it.

How to build it

The exact measurements for this project aren't included since, chances are, your mirror will vary in size from this one. But the basic steps remain the same. Head to your local home center or glass shop and buy your mirror. The edges can be beveled or plain. Once you have the mirror in hand, cut your ¼ in. plywood backer board the same size, and use that as your "stand in" mirror as you build the first part of the project.

Create the frame by joining the 1x3 sides to the 1x6 top and bottom using pocket screws (see photo 1 and sidebar). Cut crown molding—ours is about 2¼ in. wide—to fit along the top of the mirror. To avoid

splitting the small returns along the sides (photo 2), use glue and tape them in place until the glue dries.

Use glue and small brads to secure the ¼ in. plywood to the frame, making sure it's evenly spaced side-to side. Drill ½ in. dia. holes, about ½ in. deep then glue the pegs in the holes (photo 3). Add a few dabs of mirror adhesive to the back corners of the mirror, position it on the plywood and press it into place. Finally, cut and carefully nail the picture frame molding that holds the mirror to the oak frame (photo 4).

The Miraculous Pocket Screw Jig

A few years ago, the most common way of making a solid butt joint—like the type used to build the mirror frame—was to use dowels. Getting all the boards to line up and lie flush to one another was difficult—and there was no "wiggle room." If a dowel was positioned a little out of whack in any direction your frame would likewise wind up a little out of whack.

But then a clever invention came along—the pocket screw jig— which we use here. You can purchase a basic kit that contains the needed components for under $40. Here's how it works:

- Adjust the jig to the thickness of the wood. The jig is clearly marked and easily set. Since the jig is so frequently used on ¾ in. thick wood, most people just leave it set for that thickness.

- Attach the depth collar to the shank of the special drill bit. The thickness of the wood determines the position of the collar. Again the bit is clearly marked and the collar is easily adjusted.

- Center and clamp the jig to the end of the board (first photo). Bore two holes, using the hardened sleeves of the jig to guide the bit. The holes are at a very steep angle.

- Apply glue to the end of the board with the holes, position it against the other board and clamp the two together (second photo). You can buy special clamps that hold the pieces together and flat.

- Use the special long square-drive bit to drive in the special screws. The head of the screw "catches" in the bottom of the angled hole in the first board, while the shank enters the second board and cinches the two together. Different thicknesses of wood require different length screws, so make sure you use the right ones.

The joint is amazingly strong and perfect for building things like face frames for cabinets. One of the downsides to pocket screw joinery is the big, oval-shaped holes it creates. You can install special tapered plugs, but if the holes won't be seen (like with our mirror), you can leave them as is. You can buy basic and advanced kits that contain various jigs, clamps, bits, screws and plugs. We used the Kreg R3 jig ($39.99, item #22708, from Rockler; www.rockler.com).

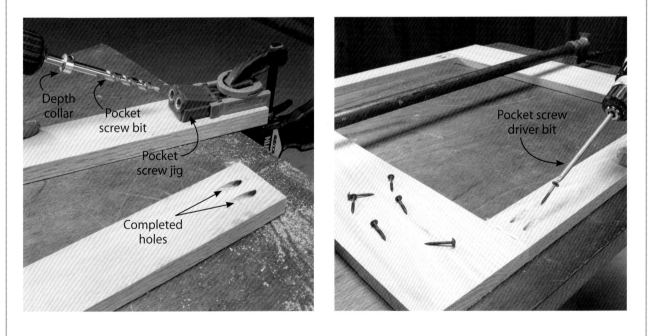

Depth collar

Pocket screw bit

Pocket screw jig

Completed holes

Pocket screw driver bit

Make a Straight-Cutting Jig

Nothing beats a tablesaw for speed and accuracy when cutting sheets of plywood or paneling. I use mine whenever I can. But still there are times I use a straight-cutting jig instead. Why? For starters, when I'm working alone, wrestling a 4x8 sheet of ¾-in plywood up onto a table saw, finding the switch, then feeding it through the saw can be a real pain—and dangerous. Sometimes I'll use my straight-cutting jig to cut panels down to manageable size and then use my tablesaw.

Other times I simply don't have room to use my table saw. When you cut an 8-ft.-long panel on a tablesaw you need at least 10 ft. of unobstructed room (8 ft. for the panel, 2 ft. for you) on each side of the saw. You need a 20 ft. clear runway for the job. A straight-cutting jig allows you to keep your panel in one place and move the saw over it, rather than vice versa.

They're so easy to construct I made an 8-ft. one for cutting long panels and a 4-ft. one for cutting shorter ones. When you're done, just stash it in the corner or on your lumber rack—try doing THAT with your tablesaw. **Tip**: paint it bright yellow so it doesn't wind up in the scrap heap.

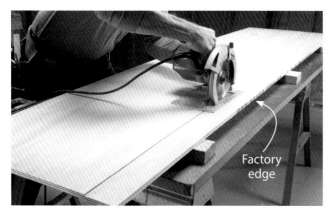

Factory edge

1 Cut a 3-in. strip of wood—one with a factory edge—from a sheet of ½-in. plywood that's at least 12 inches wide.

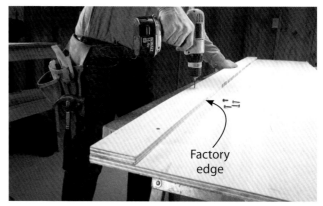

Factory edge

2 Use glue and 1-in. drywall screws to secure the strip to the remaining piece of plywood. Install it so the factory edge is facing as shown.

Scrap

Jig

3 Position the table of your circular saw against the factory edge of the 3-in. strip, then cut through the bottom piece of plywood. There's your jig.

4 Mark the board, plywood or object on each end, position the edge of your jig on those two marks, use clamps or drywall screws to hold it in place, then run the shoe of your saw along the straight edge to make the cut.

Craftsman Footstool
A clever way to make decorative cutouts in a classic cricket

Twenty-five years ago I fell in love with a small oak stool; a piece of furniture that, in its era, was often called a "cricket." Since its purchase, this Craftsman-style cricket has been used as a footstool, computer desk, kid seat, snack table and stepladder. Today, it's as attractive, useful and sturdy as the day it was built over 100 years ago. Since imitation is the most sincere form of flattery, we copied the design almost exactly.

STUFF YOU'LL NEED

1" x 12" x 4' oak	1
1" x 3" x 3' oak	1
1" x 2" x 2' oak	1

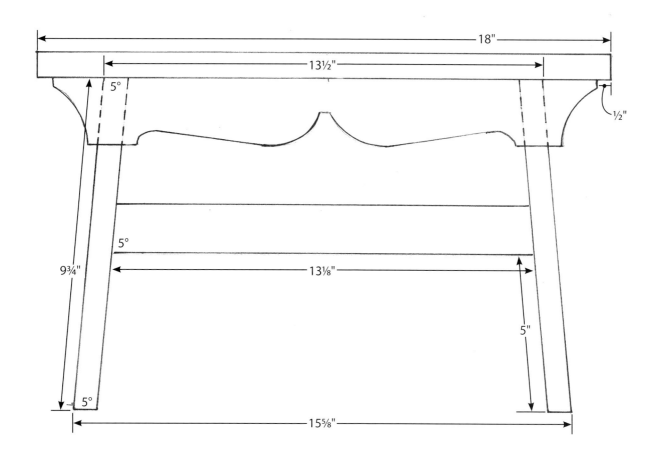

On the web

Download and print out life size patterns of the legs and crosspieces at www.ridiculouslysimplefurniture.com

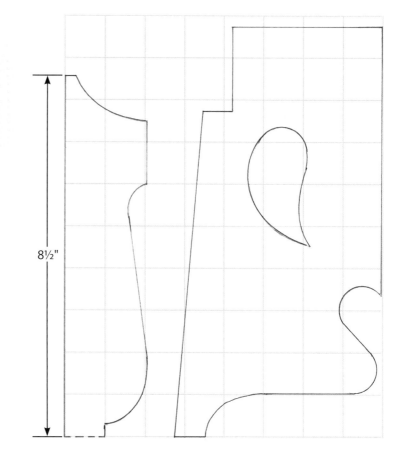

Each square = 1"

How to build it

Enlarge the half patterns for the legs and crosspieces (or printout life size versions at www.ridiculouslysimplefurniture.com), then use carbon paper to trace their "mirror image" onto the wood. Cut the profiles on the crosspieces using a jigsaw. Use a spade bit (photo 1) to create the circular parts of the teardrops and heart-shaped cutouts on the legs. Use a backer board to minimize splintering on the backside. Finish the cutouts using a thin, fine-tooth jigsaw blade. Wrap sandpaper around a short length of dowel, then smooth the inside surfaces of the cutouts.

With the legs splayed out at 5-degrees, use glue and nails to secure the crosspieces to the legs (photo 2). Create the bone-shaped cutout in the top, then place the top upside down on your work surface and position the leg assembly on top of it. Measure to make certain the leg assembly is centered on the top, then use a countersink bit to drill holes for the mounting screws. Trace around the leg assembly in a few places to create reference lines so you can reposition the leg assembly exactly. Remove the legs, apply glue to the tops of the legs and crosspieces, then reposition the leg assembly and secure it with wood screws (photo 3).

Position the stretcher as shown in photo 4, then use the countersink bit to drill two holes through each leg for those screws. If you're going to install decorative "buttons" to cover the screw heads—like we show in the opening photo—drill shallow ½-in. holes to accommodate the bases of the buttons before installing these screws.

Sand the stool, then apply stain and one coat of clear finish. Use colored putty to fill any nail holes, lightly sand again, then apply a second coat of finish.

Backer board

1 Print out or enlarge the patterns for the legs and crosspieces, then use carbon paper to transfer them onto the wood. Use a 1-in spade bit to create the upper parts of the hearts and "teardrops," then finish using a jigsaw.

2 Predrill holes, then secure the crosspieces to the legs using glue and finish nails. Make sure the legs angle out equally; there should be 12 inches between the legs at the top, 14 inches at the bottom.

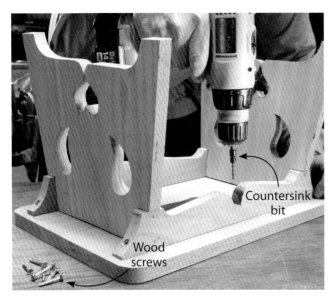

3 Apply glue to the tops of the crosspieces and use a countersink bit to predrill holes for securing the top. Use sturdy wood screws; drywall screws are likely to snap in the hard oak.

4 Install the 1" x 2" stretcher using two wood screws on each end. Install decorative buttons to conceal the screw heads.

A Little About Limbert

The footstool that inspired the project (shown here) was made by the Limbert Arts and Crafts Furniture company of Michigan. The founder, Charles Limbert, though not as well known as Gustav Stickley, exerted a great influence on the Arts and Crafts movement. Much of his furniture included the tasteful use of decorative cutouts—squares, spades, hearts (like ours) and other geometric cutouts. His sturdy, attractive furniture was so popular it was selected to furnish the Old Faithful Inn at Yellowstone National Park in 1906.

Limbert was a talented designer and progressive thinker. He also thought about the well-being of his employees; even in the early 1900s he provided indoor and outdoor recreational facilities and pleasant work environments for his workforce.

Recently, his more unique pieces have brought handsome amounts at auction, with one of his double-door bookcases selling for over $30,000. How can you tell if that rocking chair in the attic is a Limbert? Turn the piece upside down and look for a paper label or brand. If you don't find one, it doesn't mean your piece isn't a Limbert (labels and brands were often removed when a piece was refinished.) But if you do find a logo like the one shown, you may be in luck!

Plant Pedestal

A stand for elevating your plants (and woodworking skills)

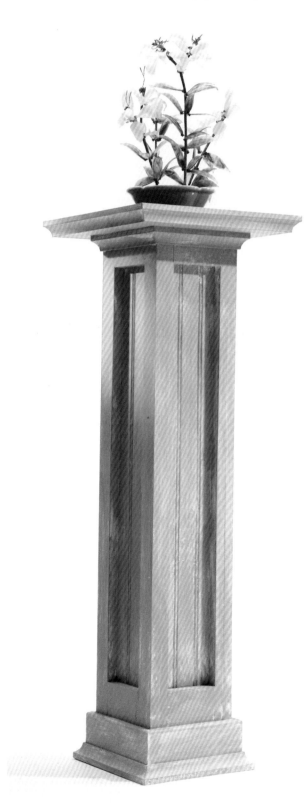

Are your plants droopy and sad? Do they just sit there day after day watching reruns of Oprah? Well perhaps they need a lift. Here's a simple solution: Raise their self-esteem by putting them on a pedestal.

A well-designed plant stand gets your plants off the floor and into the sunlight, frees up tabletops and can be an attractive addition to your décor. Here we'll show you how to build a 32-in. tall stand with a one-foot square top—but you can easily make yours taller, shorter, smaller or wider. You can also be creative with the tile inset for the top. We plopped a 12 x 12-inch marble tile in place, but you can use smaller tiles and grout the seams.

STUFF YOU'LL NEED

¾" x ¾" x 6' pine	2
¾" x 1½" x 6' pine	2
¾" x 3½" x 4' pine	1
¾" x 7¼" x 3' pine	1
¼" x 3" x 8' beadboard	2
¾" cove molding	13 li. ft.
½" x 12" x 12" plywood	1
12" x 12" tile	1

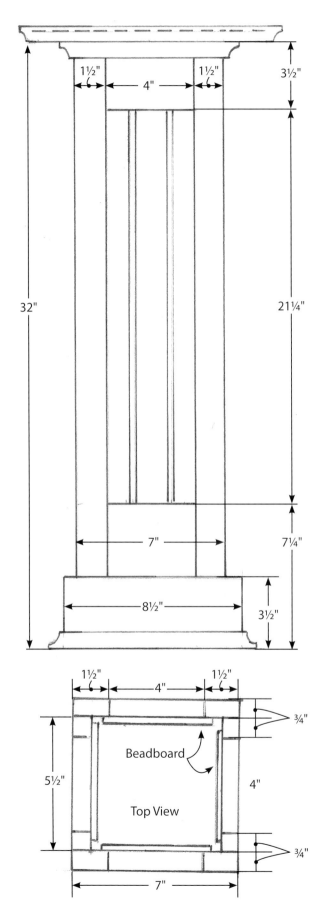

How to build it

This plant stand is basically four rectangular panels joined together to form a box, with trim pieces added to finish it off.

Build the four frames (photo 1). Note that one pair is slightly wider than the other pair. Secure the bead board to the backsides of the frames using brads (photo 2). Attach the four panels to one another using 6d finish nails and carpentry glue (photo 3). Before the glue dries, place your Speed Square on one end to check if the box is square. If it's not, use a clamp to squeeze the opposite corners until it is square.

Attach the top plywood platform with glue and finish nails. Glue and nail cove molding to the edges of the plywood and to the top and base of the pedestal (photo 4). Plop the tile in place (photo 5). You can use silicone caulk to hold the tile in place and fill the small gaps between the edges of the tile and the trim pieces if you want.

Paint or finish the stand to protect it from moisture; it's bound to get a shower at some point while someone is watering the plant.

1 Cut the pieces to length, then use glue and finish nails to assemble the four frames. Note, two frames will have ¾-in.-wide side pieces and two will have 1½-wide side pieces.

2 Cut the bead board to length and use short brads to nail the boards to the backs of the frames. On the two frames with the widest side pieces, hold the bead board back at least ⅞-in. from the edges.

3 Glue and nail the frames to one another to create the pedestal. Use a small square to make certain the "box" is square.

4 Add the 1x4s and trim pieces to the base of the pedestal. Cut the pieces a little long, mark them in place as shown, cut them to final length, then glue and nail them in place.

5 Secure a piece of plywood, ⅛-in larger than the tile you intend to put on top, to the pedestal, making sure it's centered. Add cove molding wide enough to cover the edge of the plywood and tile. Plop the tile in place.

Staining, Clear Finishes and Paintball Guns

The finish on a project can make or break the way it looks. You can meticulously build a Craftsman-style stool from beautiful oak, but if the finish looks like it's been applied with a paintball gun you've wasted a lot of time and wood.

Selecting a finish shouldn't be an afterthought; in fact it should be a "before thought." Before even buying your wood, select the finish. If your table is going to be painted, there's no need buying expensive oak; you could save time and money using pine or plywood. But if that table is going to have a clear finish, you'll want to select your boards carefully, then position them with the best sides showing. You'll want to carefully remove excess glue as you work so the glue doesn't create blotches in the final finish. You'll want to position your fasteners strategically so they won't distract.

For some people, applying the finish is their favorite part of the project; the payoff pitch for all the work that's come before. I'm not one of them. I adhere to the physician's motto, "Above all, do no harm." After I drive my last nail, my goal is to apply a finish that enhances the look of the wood while protecting the piece—without taking too much time.

Entire books have been written on applying clear finishes, so we're not going to be able to even begin scratching the surface (har, har) here. But in my mind, there are three really important things to know:

1) Before staining or finishing any project, experiment on a scrap of wood from the project. Apply the finish to the end grain and face grain to see if it behaves differently. Label your test blocks and store them somewhere; they'll come in handy for future projects.

2) If you're going to stain pine, apply sanding sealer first. Different parts of the board—the end grain, areas around knots, places where the grain changes direction—absorb stains at different rates, often creating a blotchy appearance. Sanding sealer fills the open pores that cause this blotchiness so finishes apply more uniformly (top photo).

3) Danish oil is one of the easiest, most forgiving finishes to apply on hardwoods. You can purchase it in a variety of tints, apply it with a rag, and apply multiple coats to deepen the color and build a protective coat (bottom photo).

Maple boards (left) and pine boards (right) that have been stained without sanding sealer (top boards) and with sealer (bottom). Sanding sealer evens out the absorption rate to provide a more uniform look.

Oak scraps with three kinds of finishes applied. The shellac (left) imparts a mellow orangish tint; the natural Danish oil (center) enriches the grain and offers moderate protection; high-gloss polyurethane creates a shiny, protective coat.

TIP ★ *Beware of Spontaneous Combustion*

A pile of oily rags can generate enough heat to spontaneously burst into flames. If you use rags or paper towels to apply Danish oil, linseed oil or other oil based products, lay them outside to dry out before tossing them.

Stack-'Em-Up Cubes

Build 'em, stack 'em, use 'em anyway you want

Life changes—so do our storage needs, possessions and room sizes. One day your kid needs toy storage, the next a place to stash clothes, the next, it's "Hey dad can I bring a coupla those cubie things to college?" That's why these modular cubes are so handy. You can build as many as you want and stack them any way you want. You can build simple cubes or add drawers, shelves, partitions and doors. They're sturdy, yet small and easy to cart around. And they're cheap—about $8 per cube.

STUFF YOU'LL NEED / UNIT

¾" x 10" x 5' particle board shelving	1
¼" x 15" x 15" plywood	1

How to build them

You could (and still can) simply cut the box components to length and nail the corners together. But cutting rabbets on the ends creates stronger boxes, and cutting dadoes in the middle creates stronger shelves and partitions. To cut accurate, consistent size grooves, use a straight cutting jig like the one we show in building the "Which End's Up?" bookcase. Make a series of cuts to create the ¼-in. deep, ¾-in.-wide groove (photo 1), then push a sharp ¾-in. chisel through the groove to remove the waste and flatten the bottom. Use a scrap piece of shelf material to make sure the rabbets and dadoes are wide enough.

Use white glue and finish nails to secure the box sides and any partitions in place (photo 2.) The tighter the fit, the better. Before the glue dries, check the box for squareness (photo 3) and install the ¼-in.-plywood back.

Make it your own

It's easy to customize your cubes to meet your storage needs.

If you want cubes with **doors**, cut panels from ¾-in. plywood and install them with small hinges. Put a stop block on the inside of the box so the door can't swing in too far.

If you want cubes with **drawers**, build simple boxes with rabbeted corners and add ¼-in. plywood to the bottom. Picture frame the front with molding to cover the plywood bottom and add a decorative detail. Add a pull.

If you want cubes with vertical or horizontal **partitions**, cut extra dado grooves in the box sides before assembling them.

Trim

Plywood bottom

1 Use a simple straight cutting jig to cut the rabbets on the ends of the boards and the dadoes in the middle. Make a series of 5 or 6 cuts, moving the jig as you work, then use a ¾-in. chisel to remove the waste.

2 Use glue and nails to secure the corners of the box and any partitions. Tight joints make for better strength and appearance.

3 Measure the diagonals; lightly squeeze the corners of the box until the two measurements are equal. (That means your box is square.) Add ¼-in. plywood to the back to keep it square.

Television Console

A kitchen cabinet lies at the heart of this surprisingly easy-to-build project

This project may look out of your league, but the hardest part has already been built for you. The heart and soul of this entertainment center is actually a 36-in. wide wall cabinet purchased at Lowe's for 35 bucks; the rest is just plywood, boards and moldings. Some people might consider using a store-bought cabinet cheating; I consider it a smart way to build a decent-looking entertainment center in an afternoon.

Since cabinets vary in size, and you may wish to make your center larger or smaller, exact dimensions aren't included. But follow the basic steps and think a step ahead and your project will be a success. Many amplifiers, tuners, game consoles and other components are over 12 inches deep (the depth of our store-bought cabinet), so we used plywood to increase the depth to fifteen inches. You can make yours deeper or shallower according to your needs.

STUFF YOU'LL NEED

Upper wall cabinet (ours was 12" deep, 15" tall, 30" wide)

¾" oak plywood

1x2, 1x3 and 1x4 oak

1x3 pine

¾" cove molding

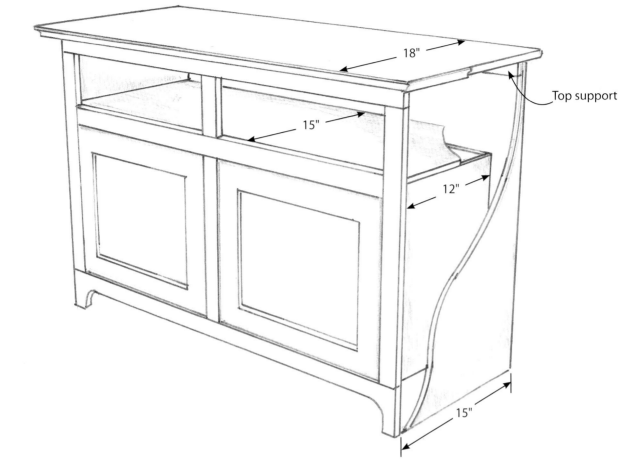

18"

15"

12"

Top support

15"

How to build it

Begin by furring out the two sides of the cabinet with scraps of ¼-in. plywood. This will make the sides of the cabinet even with the "ears" of the face frame so the plywood will lay flat. Temporarily prop up the cabinet on some 2x4s, then use glue and nails to secure the plywood sides to the cabinet (photo 1). The plywood will extend below the cabinet to accommodate the base trim and above the cabinet to accommodate the open shelf and top.

Cut the four components of the face frame—the two long horizontal and two vertical members—to size and lay them on the cabinet to check the fit (photo 2). You want the "reveal" (a fancy word for gap) between this frame and doors to be equal all the way around, so cut and adjust the components until they fit right—then glue and nail them in place. Start with the long horizontal 1x4 bottom piece (cut the arch in it first), then install the long horizontal top piece, followed by the two side pieces.

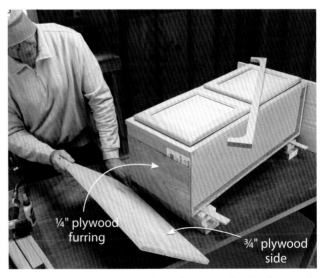

¼" plywood furring

¾" plywood side

1 Fur out the sides of the cabinet with ¼" plywood, then add the ¾" oak plywood sides to increase the depth and height of the cabinet.

Cut and install the shelf that rests on top of your store-bought cabinet (photo 3), then install the horizontal 1x2 that covers the raw edge of this piece of plywood and top edge of the cabinet. Remember, you want the reveal between this piece and the tops of the doors to be the same size as the reveals around the other sides of the doors. Cut and install the vertical member between the doors; you may need to rip this lengthwise to maintain an even reveal around the doors. Then install the shorter divider directly above it.

Nail a long horizontal support piece across the back of the cabinet (between the plywood sides) to support the top. Install the top making sure it overhangs the cabinet equally on both sides (in our case 1 inch). Use glue and nails to secure it in place. Finally, cut and install the cove molding around the front and sides of the top.

Stain, finish, connect and relax.

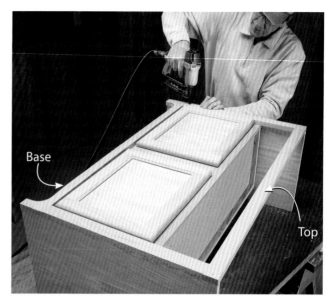

2 Cut and nail the face frame members to the face of the cabinet and edges of the plywood. Install the 1x2 that spans across the top of the open compartment.

3 Cut and secure a piece of ¾" plywood to cover the top of the cabinet and create the bottom shelf for the open upper compartment.

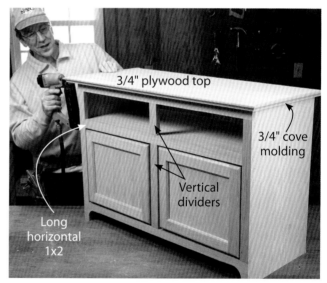

4 Secure the long horizontal 1x2 that covers the edge of the plywood and upper edge of the cabinet. Install the vertical divider between the doors, then another divider directly above it in the open compartment. Glue and nail the long horizontal piece to support the back of the top, then install the ¾" plywood top and ¾" cove molding to cover the plywood edges.

Leaning Ladder Shelf
Buy one for $299—or build one for $30

Browsing through the catalog of a popular home furnishings company, I came across a shelf system identical to this one in nearly every respect, but one: The $299 price tag. Plus shipping. This leaning ladder bookshelf—made entirely from standard size lumber—provides shelves of five different depths and costs 90% less. Since the shelves are screwed to the ladder rails, it's easy to disassemble and pack when it's time to move. And if you're tool deprived, you can build the entire thing using only a jigsaw, hammer and drill.

Stuff You'll Need	
1" x 3" x 8'	7
1" x 4" x 3'	1
1" x 6" x 3'	1
1" x 8" x 3'	1
1" x 10" x 3'	1
1" x 12" x 3'	1

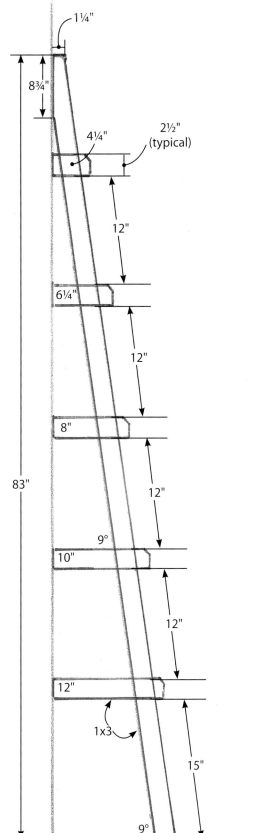

1¼"

8¾"

4¼"

2½"
(typical)

12"

6¼"

12"

83"

8"

12"

9°

10"

12"

12"

1x3

15"

9°

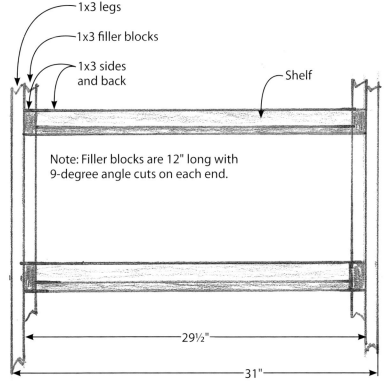

1x3 legs

1x3 filler blocks

1x3 sides
and back

Shelf

Note: Filler blocks are 12" long with
9-degree angle cuts on each end.

29½"

31"

Front View Detail

How to build it

If you're going to paint your shelf system, do it before
you assemble it. Also, add about ¹⁄₁₆ in. to the width of
the spacer block used in photo 1. That little extra space
will provide room for the thickness of the paint, so you
don't have to bang your shelves into the slots.

Make sure to build the ladder sides so they're the
mirror image of one another (photo 1). Secure the back
and sides to each shelf (photo 2) using glue and 2-in.
nails. This is a project where a nail gun comes in really
handy since there are over 30 different parts involved.

2 Build the shelf units using one 1x4, 1x6, 1x8, 1x10 and 1x12 for the shelves and 1x3s for the back and sides. Use glue and 2-in. nails for fasteners.

1 Cut the ladder "rails" as shown in the illustration, then add the 12-in.-long filler blocks. Use a scrap piece of 1x3 as a spacer to make sure the slots are wide enough to accommodate the shelf units.

3 Position one rail so the angled top lies flat against the work surface. Set the uppermost and lowermost shelves in place and secure them to the rail so they extend 1" beyond the front of the rail. Add the remaining shelves, then repeat on the other side. Use clamps to temporarily position the shelves if necessary.

Assemble your shelf unit on a large flat surface (photo 3). Install the widest (lowest) and skinniest (highest) shelves first, then install the shelves in between, making sure the backs of all the shelves sit flat on your work surface.

The unit can stand on its own, but if you have little kids, climbing cats or rowdy parties, you may want to drive a couple of screws through the back of one of the upper shelves into wall studs for added stability.

A Word on Woods

You know those 1x4s you buy? You've probably noticed they aren't one by four of anything. They may have started out that size, but by the time they've been dried, planed and processed those dimensions have changed. You've also probably noticed there are two or three types of 1x4s in the store. They can vary by both grade and species.

These photos provide some basic information.

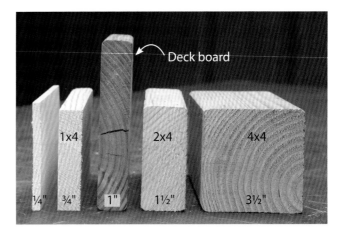

Thickness

Lumber also has a nominal and actual thickness. Boards referred to as 1 x (something) are usually ¾ in. thick, boards referred to as 2 x (something) are usually 1½ inches thick, and 4x4s are usually 3½ inches in each dimension. Deck boards—sometimes referred to as 4/4 or 5/4 boards—can vary in thickness from ⅞ inch to 1⅛ inch. Boards thinner than ¾ inch are usually the thickness the name implies; a board labeled "½ inch" is, indeed, usually ½ inch thick.

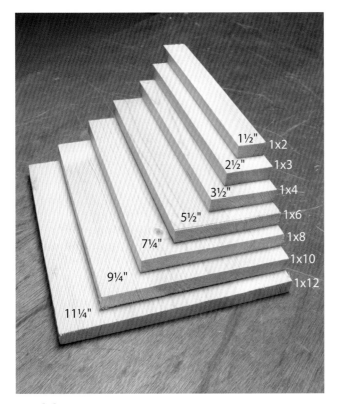

Width

Boards have a "nominal" and an "actual" width. Nominal is the name used to describe the wood in the lumberyard (1x12, 2x4, etc), while actual is the true dimension of the board. As a rule of thumb, subtract ¾ inch from the nominal width of boards that are 1x6 through 1x12 to get their actual width, and ½ inch from boards that are 1x2 through 1x6 .

Grade

Boards are graded based on the number and size of knots and other defects. It can get very complicated when it comes to structural and hardwood lumber, and can also be complicated with pine boards since different home centers and lumberyards have different names for the different grades. But for our intents and purposes we'll keep it simple. You'll usually find two or three grades in pine boards:

#3, standard or construction grade boards cost the least, but have the most knots and other defects, and are more likely to be warped, cupped or bowed. This is okay for some projects, but for others you'll wind up fighting with the defects the entire way.

#2 or quality boards have small knots and other defects, but have a decent appearance and are structurally sound. They're good for shelving and projects that are painted.

#1, premium or select boards have few (or no) knots and other defects. You'll pay a premium—three or four times what you'd pay for other grades—but they're easier to work with and have excellent appearance.

Species: Interior Wood

When you dive into the world of hardwood and exotic lumber, you'll find hundreds of species; when you dive into your local home center, you'll most likely find these three woods:

Maple is moderately hard, moderately priced and stains with moderate success. Its light crisp appearance makes it popular for cabinetry and furniture.

Oak is moderately priced, harder than maple, often has interesting grain figure and stains like a dream. The wood has been favored by cabinetmakers and furniture makers for years.

Pine is the softest of the three; it's easy to work, widely available and—at least in the lower grades—relatively inexpensive.

Species: Exterior Wood

There are many woods that can stand up to the elements—redwood, cypress, teak, even regular old pine if it's properly painted and maintained. But at most lumberyards you'll find these two choices:

Treated pine is inexpensive, long lasting and structurally sound, making it ideal for outdoor projects. It can be stained, but left to its own devices it will turn silvery gray in a few years. Buy dry wood (you can tell a lot by the feel and weight). Wet wood is more likely to shrink leaving gaps in your project.

The new generation of ACQ and CA treated lumber is safer than the old CCA treated lumber, but you should still take precautions. Wear a dust mask and eye protection when working with it (as you would with other lumber), but also wear gloves, wash your hands after handling it, don't burn scraps and don't

use it where it will come in direct contact with drinking water. For more information, read the supplier's information sheets.

Cedar has a rich "woodsy-folksy" look and is moderately priced. It's not as strong as treated pine, but is fine for most small furniture projects. Finishing it with a clear preservative or exterior finish will help it preserve its rich look for years.

Real Hardwood Lumber Stores

Real hardwood lumberyards—places where you find exotic woodworkers meticulously picking through stacks of exotic wood—play by different rules when it comes to lumber dimensions and pricing. Boards are often sold "rough sawn" (they haven't been run through a planer) and their thickness is spelled out in quarters of an inch. For example, a one-inch thick board is really and truly one inch thick and referred to as 4/4; a one-and-a-half-inch thick board is called 6/4 and so on. Lumber is sold this way because serious woodworkers have planers, joiners, tablesaws and wide belt sanders that help them create boards the exact dimensions they need.

There are some other terms you'll encounter if you visit a hardwood lumber dealer:

RS: The board is rough sawn; it hasn't been planed and there are saw tooth marks on it.

S2S: The board has been planed on both faces, but the edges are rough

S3S: The board has been planed on 3 surfaces; both faces and one edge have been planed, but one edge is rough.

S4S: The board has been planed on four surfaces; both faces and both edges have been planed.

BF: Lumber price is based on board foot. To calculate how many board feet (bf) there are in a board, multiply thickness (in inches) by width (in inches) by length (in feet), then divide by 12. For example, to calculate how many board feet there are in a 6/4 (1½-in.) thick board that's 8 inches wide and six feet long you'd perform this calculation:

- 6/4 x 8 =12
- 12 x 6 = 72
- 72 divided by 12 = 6 bf

If the wood was $7.25/bf, you'd write out a check for $43.50.

Magazine & Book Rack

One way it stores your favorite magazines, the other way it displays your favorite book

Are your magazines homeless? Do they drift aimlessly from mailbox to coffee table to nightstand to bathroom floor? Perhaps the solution lies in building this simple rack. It will easily hold two dozen magazines "spine up" so they're easy to find and it fits nicely next to a reading chair. You can even slide it apart for easy storing and moving.

Another unique feature is that it can be converted into an attractive book or dictionary display rack by simply sliding it apart and crossing its legs in the other direction.

How to build it

Cut the 1x12 to length, then mark the locations of the ¾-in.-wide slots. Set your jigsaw at 22½-degrees and make pairs of cuts (photo 1) that are 5¾ in. long (just a hair over half the width of the 1x12). Use a sharp chisel to make the end cut of the notch. Test fit the two pieces by sliding the grooves together. If they don't slide together easily, carefully widen the cuts with sandpaper or your jigsaw.

Flex a thin piece of metal or wood into a gentle curve (photo 2) and trace the profile onto all four edges of the board; the sides and bottom will be concave, the top will be convex. Use either a helper or screws to hold the wood or metal strip as you trace around it. Mark and cut one board, then use that as a template for tracing the same pattern onto the other board.

Sand the edges smooth. If you have a belt sander, use it. If not, wrap sandpaper around one of the cut-offs to create a curved sanding block and sand away. Slightly round and soften the edges so they're not so

STUFF YOU'LL NEED

1" x 12" x 3'	1

1 Cut ¾-in.-wide notches into both boards using a jigsaw set at 22½ degrees. Use a sharp ¾-in. chisel to remove the waste piece. Test fit the boards.

2 Flex a thin piece of wood or metal and trace the edge to mark the curved sides, top and bottom. Clamp the boards to your work surface as you cut the curves with your jigsaw.

Curved sanding block

3 Sand the edges smooth. If you don't have a power sander, wrap sandpaper around the edge of a curved cutout and press hard as you work. Rout the edges if you wish.

sharp; if you have a router, you can use a roundover bit to do this.

Stain the two boards, then apply 2 coats of clear finish. To set it up in magazine mode, slide the pieces together so the X-shape is vertical. For book display mode, nest the boards the opposite direction to create a more horizontal X-shape.

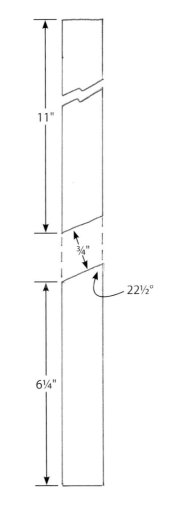

11"

¾"

22½°

6¼"

Floating Wall Shelf
Look ma, no brackets!

Your flaky Aunt Patty might call this a mystical levitating shelf. Engineers might call it a torsion box. I call it a clever use for that old bifold door sitting in the basement.

This shelf works on the torsion box principle. A torsion box is basically two "skins" applied to both sides of a lightweight core to create a surprisingly solid structure; one strong enough to be used to build airplane wings. In this case, the bifold door—with its two thin layers of plywood applied over a honeycomb cardboard core—is a torsion box searching for a purpose.

> ### STUFF YOU'LL NEED
> Bifold door
>
> 1" x 2" pine (for filler strip and mounting cleats)
>
> Base cap molding
>
> ¼" x 3" lag bolts

How to build it

Begin by using your straight-cutting jig (see p. 27) to cut the bifold door to size. You can rip it right down the middle to create two 80-in.-long shelves, or offset your cut to make shelves that are wider or narrower. Rip a 1x2 to the thickness of the door's core—about 1⅛ in.—using your circular saw or table saw. Cut, glue and nail part of this filler strip into the open end of the door (photo 2). Set aside another piece to be used later as the wall mounting strip. If your shelves are long or need to support extra weight, rip down a 2x4 instead of a 1x4 so you have a heavier-duty mounting cleat.

Install moldings along the three shelf sides. We used 1½-in.-wide base cap molding, but you can use other moldings or thin strips of wood. If you're going to paint your shelves, you can even leave the shelf edges plain.

Select the location for your shelf, locate the wall studs, then use lag bolts, at least 3-in. long, to secure the mounting strip to the studs. The mounting strip should be just a little shorter than the opening in the back of the shelf. Predrill holes in the strip so it doesn't split.

1 Use a straight-cut jig to cut a hollow core bifold door lengthwise, then to the desired length. Cut the door "good face down" to minimize chipping.

2 Glue and nail a filler block into the open end. The cleat that you'll use for mounting the shelf to the wall will be the same thickness as the filler block, so cut them both at the same time.

Apply glue to the top and bottom of the cleat, then slip the shelf over it and have a helper hold the shelf tightly against the wall. Use a short torpedo level—or an iPhone with the "iHandy Level" app—to make sure the shelf is level; maybe even tilted up a degree or two. Use 1-in. drywall screws to secure the shelf to the underlying cleat on both the top and bottom. Prop it up with scrap 2x4s until the glue dries.

> **TIP ★ One Little Problem**
>
> There's one big downside to this shelf: Since the shelf is glued to the cleat, there's no good way of removing it without demolishing the shelf. So make sure you know exactly where you want it.

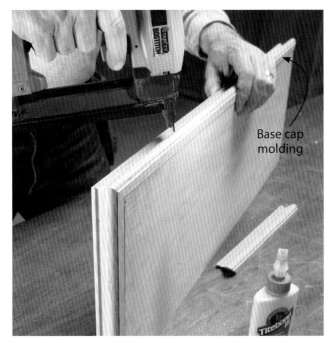

3 Install decorative moldings along the edges. We used base cap, which is the same thickness as the door, but you can use any size or shape molding you want. If you'll be painting the door, you can leave the edges unfinished.

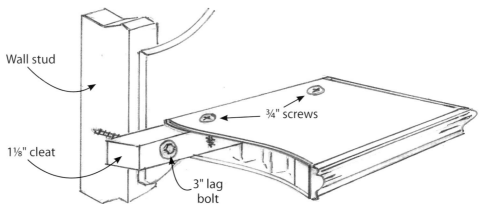

Entertainment Pantry

A ridiculously simple way to make raised panel doors—and store Guitar Hero and Wii paraphernalia, plus DVDs

This storage cabinet is modeled after those ingenious kitchen pantry cabinets that swing, glide, rollout and seemingly hold three decade's worth of canned goods. This pantry has room for 100s of DVDs, CDs and boxed sets, and the top is just the right size for a mid-size television or sound system. Eliminate some of the shelves and you have the perfect storage place for Guitar Hero, Wii and other game accessories. The key to being able to cram so much stuff into this little cabinet is that the doors can store nearly as much stuff as the cabinet itself.

Don't let the raised panel doors scare you away—they're made from a bifold door cut into two smaller panels. We installed shelves to accommodate both DVDs and CDs, but you can adjust the spacing to hold video game equipment, books, board games or whatever you want.

How to build it

Building this storage pantry involves constructing three boxes, then securing them to one another using piano hinges.

Cut the 12-in.-wide bifold door into two equal size panels (photo 1). Since you can't buy a "monofold" door, you're going to wind up with an extra door that you can use to build a second cabinet or give to some other aspiring cabinetmaker. You may not be able to buy the exact size door we did (ours was a colonial style, raised panel door made by Classic Décor), so you may need to modify the measurements we show a bit—but the basic construction details remain the same.

Build two boxes from 1x6s that are ⅛-in. smaller in both directions than the cabinet doors. Then secure the cabinet doors to the boxes using 6d finish nails and glue (photo 2).

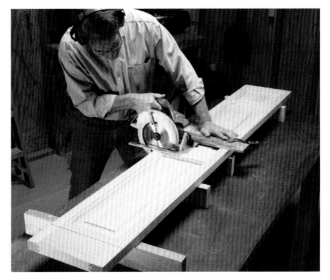

1 Measure and mark the bifold door so you can cut it into two equal-size panels. Make sure the top and bottom stiles are of equal size on both doors. Clamp a straight edge in place, so when you guide your saw base along it, the blade will cut along the marked lines.

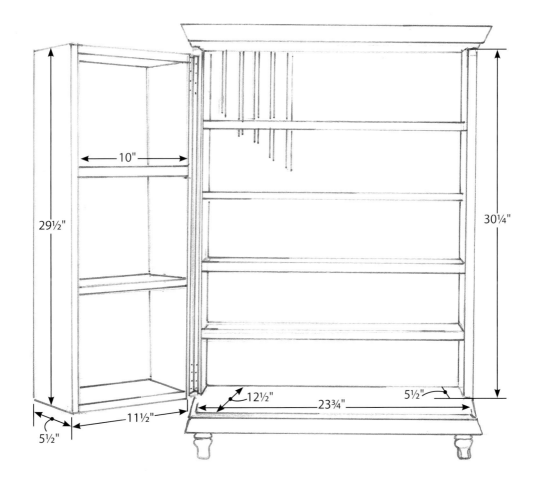

Lay the two door units side-by-side. The next box you build needs to be able to accommodate these two doors, but you need to make this cabinet body ⅛ inch wider and ½ inch taller than the doors so they have room to swing. Nail the 1x6s to the plywood top and bottom as shown (photo 3). Make sure the box is square (see the sidebar), then glue and nail the ⅜-in. bead board to the back (photo 4). You can use plywood if you want.

Position the cabinet on a large flat surface and place the doors on either side. Prop up the cabinet so the edges are even with those of the door (photo 5).

Install three hinge screws (top, bottom and middle) in each side of each box, then carefully stand the unit up and see how the doors fit when closed. You can slightly raise, lower or angle the hinges to make the doors close more evenly. Install the rest of the screws.

Glue and nail the bifold stop molding along the top and bottom edges of the cabinet (photo 6). Install the 1x6 shelves according to what you'll be storing inside. For CDs, you need at least 5 inches of "headroom"; for DVDs, you need at least 8 inches. Install the feet, pulls and magnetic latch. Finish the cabinet with paint, stain or a clear finish.

2 Build two boxes ⅛-in. smaller in both directions than the doors. Glue and nail the doors to these boxes, so the boxes are inset just a hair.

3 Build the cabinet so it can accommodate both doors when they're closed. The top and bottom are plywood; the sides are 1x6s. "Square it up" as explained in the sidebar.

4 Install the bead board backing using glue and nails. You can substitute plywood if you wish.

5 Prop up the cabinet so the hinge surfaces are even. Install a few hinge screws, then stand up your cabinet to see how the doors meet when closed. Adjust the hinges as necessary, then drive in the rest of the screws.

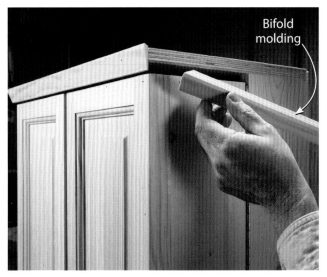

TIP ★ *Pick 'Em Straight*

Sight down the edges of the 1x6s at the lumberyard or home center and pick nice straight ones. This way, when you build your cabinet and cabinet door boxes, they'll be nice and straight. If you use warped or bowed materials you'll have difficulty making your doors line up when closed.

6 Install the bifold molding. This does two things: It covers the edges of plywood and it makes the gap between the doors and plywood top and bottom smaller.

How to "Square Things Up"

Lots of times in the book you'll be told to "square things up" before moving on to the next step. You need to "square things up" no matter how big or little the thing is you're building—whether it's a little cabinet or a 40-foot-long wall when you're building a new house.

The best way to "square things up" is to take two diagonal measurements (from corner to corner) and adjust the box or frame until these two measurements are equal. With small projects you simply squeeze the long measurement just a little bit to equal things up; remember as you shorten the length of one diagonal, you'll be increasing the length of another—so don't over do it. Keep checking and adjusting until the measurements are equal.

Once something is square, you need to keep it square. Sometimes you can do this by simply holding the piece with clamps or a couple of temporary nails while the glue sets; other times you'll keep it square by nailing plywood or metal brackets to the piece. In this case we'll hold it square by nailing the bead board to the back.

If you're dealing with a box or frame that has glued joints, you need to "square things up" ASAP or else you risk weakening the glued joints as you adjust the sides.

Nomad Laptop Desk

A fold-up, portable desk for working on the go—or in bed

This little desk is for those who like to work spread out on the floor or use their bed for an office. It's the right height for working comfortably while seated on the floor, and is tall enough so you can slide your legs under it while working in bed. The amoeba-shape top is large enough to hold a laptop plus a few odds and ends, and the legs fold in so when you're done you can stash it behind a chair or under the bed. It also makes a great sawed off TV tray for those who like to eat breakfast, lunch or dinner (or all three) in bed.

Stuff You'll Need	
¾" x 2' x 2' plywood	1
1" x 2" x 8 ft. pine board	1
24" piano hinge	1
Flexible dentil molding	2 packs
(Molding available at www.rockler.com)	

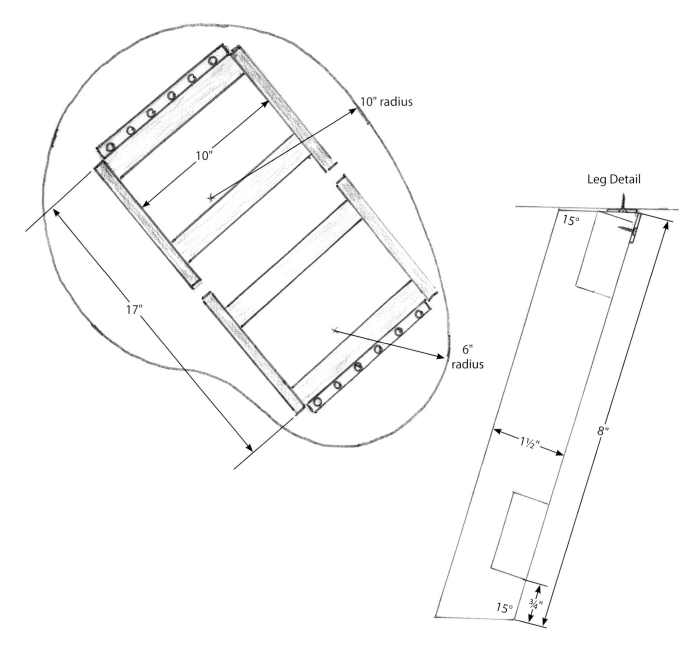

Leg Detail

10" radius

10"

17"

6" radius

15°

1½"

8"

15°   ¾"

How to build it

The desktop can be any shape you want, as long as it's big enough to accommodate your computer on top and the folding legs underneath. We based our design on two large circles joined by two curves, and sized it so it could be cut from a 2 x 2-ft. sheet of plywood.

Draw the two circles, then trace along the edge of a bent strip of wood to create a curve that gradually joins them (photo 1). Use a jigsaw to cut out the shape (photo 2), staying a little outside the line so you can sand up to the line to get the exact shape.

Install the flexible molding using glue and small brads (photo 3). Use a needle nose pliers to hold the brad so you don't whap your fingers. You'll use two

sections, so put the final joint where they meet in a place that's least conspicuous.

When you build the legs, pay particular attention to the position of the top crosspiece (or else your hinges won't work properly). Mark out the location of the legs on the top. Position them so they won't bang into one another when folded. Cut the piano hinge to the same length as the crosspieces, using a hack saw. Screw the hinge first to the upper crosspiece and then to the desk bottom (photo 4). The heads of the brass screws strip out easily, so avoid frustration and pre-drill the holes.

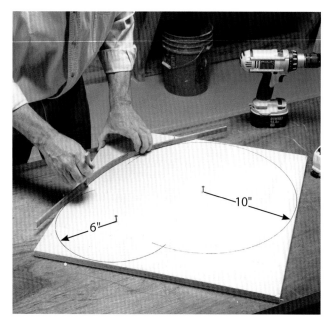

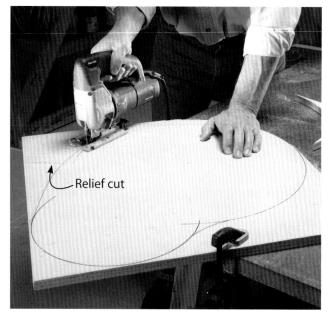

1 Draw the desktop shape onto your plywood. You can use our dimensions or design your own. If your plywood has a "good" and "bad" side, mark your pattern on the bad side.

2 Use a jigsaw with a fine tooth blade to cut out the shape. Make a few "relief cuts" as shown so the scrap pieces fall off every once in a while. Use a sanding block or power sander to smooth the edges.

3 Use glue and ¾-in. brads to secure the flexible molding to the edge of the desktop.

4 Cut the leg and cross pieces to the right angle and length, then pre-build the leg units. Install them using piano hinges.

TIP ★ *Edging Options*

We used store-bought, flexible molding for the edging—but other materials will work just as well. Iron-on veneer tape is one economical option. Plastic edging is also available. You can also use a thin strip of solid wood; pre-soaking it in hot water in your bathtub with a little fabric softener added will make it more flexible.

The Zen of Jigsawing

If you were stranded on a desert island—one with electricity—and you could have just one power saw, you'd be wise to choose a jigsaw. Circular saws may cut faster and straighter, bandsaws may cut curves with more accuracy, reciprocating saws may be able to cut weird materials in weird places—but jigsaws can handle all of these tasks with above-passing grades. Plus they're safe. While some people are terrified by the whirring and whining of a circular saw, most people find the up and down movement of a jigsaw downright folksy.

A Few Basics

- Keep a variety of blades in your arsenal. Those with coarse teeth (fewer TPI or teeth-per-inch) and wide blades cut aggressively, but can't make tight turns. Fine tooth blades are usually thinner and cut slower, but can cut very tight radiuses; they also break easier.

- When accuracy is important, cut just to the outside of your line, then use a power sander to remove material precisely up to the line.

- When cutting out a large complex shape, create a series of relief cuts running from the edge of the board to the edge of the shape so scrap pieces fall away in smaller pieces. Also, make relief cuts where the shape has tight or sharp-angled inside corners, so your blade has more room to turn and maneuver.

- Make sure your blade doesn't run into the underlying work surface; if it does you'll bend your blade and the saw may fly up toward you with a sudden jolt.

- Brush or blow sawdust away from the cut line so you can see it clearly. Some tools even have a built-in dust blower.

Cut with your whole body

Cutting accurately requires Zen-like patience and focus. Lean lightly into the saw and move your whole upper body along with your arm when cutting large curves. Don't force the saw.

Hold on tight

Use your hand, knee, clamp or combinations thereof to hold the board securely down onto a solid surface. The saw cuts on the up-stroke, pulling the board against the base of the jigsaw.

Drill starter holes

When making a cutout in the middle of a board, drill a starter hole for your jigsaw blade. Some starter holes—like the ones for the teardrop cutouts shown here—can both create an entry point for the blade and create part of the cutout itself.

Guide it

Use a square or straight edge to guide the edge of your jigsaw table to create straight cuts.

Which End's Up? Bookshelves

A trio of trapezoids you can arrange to create shelves, desk or ???

These trapezoid bookshelves can be used for lots of different things and be arranged in lots of different ways. You can position them upside down, right-side up and side-by-side to create bookshelves. You can use two to create a desk. You can even use them individually as plant pedestals or display stands.

One of the keys to success is to buy boards that are straight and flat. Those with cups and curves will be a hassle to join at the corners. And the shelf units won't fit snugly against one another.

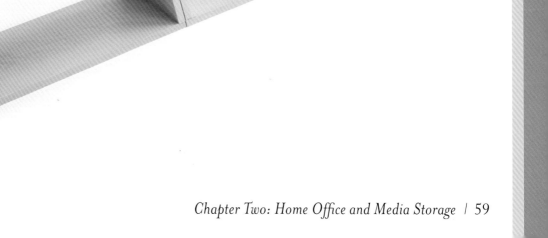

How to build it

If you have access to a sliding compound miter saw or radial arm saw, by all means use one to make the angled cuts. Otherwise build the crosscut jig described in the sidebar; it will help you make straight, quick, square cuts. Use 10-ft.-long boards, since the angled cut from the previously cut shelf part can be used for the angled end cut on the next part (photo 1).

Use 2-in. drywall screws to join the 1x10s that form the main tapezoid. When you install the intermediate shelf (photo 2), make sure not to bow the sides in or out. The trapezoids are fairly rigid, but if you're going to move them around a lot or subject them to lots of weight install a ¼-in.-thick plywood back for rigidity.

You can set up your bookshelf units as they are, or jazz them up. We built a top out of ¾-in. plywood edged with moldings to create a continuous (and more attractive) bookshelf top.

The desktop (next page) is also just ¾-in. plywood with moldings applied to the edges. You can make the top any length or width you want (within reason). Just make certain the top is rigid enough to hold all your stuff.

1 Cut the boards to the correct length at a 16-degree angle, using your crosscut jig (see sidebar). Flip the board over after cutting each piece and you'll get a "free" end cut for the next board.

2 Assemble the outer frame using glue and nails, then install the middle shelf, making sure you don't force the sides out or in. You can make this shelf longer or shorter if you prefer a different spacing.

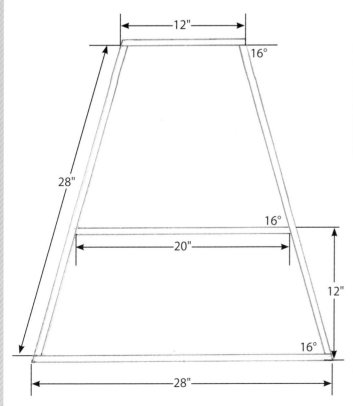

12"
16°
28"
16°
20"
16°
12"
16°
28"

Note: You must use these dimensions, or the 16 degree measurement will change.

Make it your own

These trapezoids can be arranged in a lot of different ways.

- Place ¾-in. plywood across two units to create a desk. Add trim to cover the exposed edges.
- Use wider or narrower boards if you prefer wider or narrower shelves.
- Place a long continuous board across the tops to hold the units together and create a more uniform look (like we did). Add trim for an even more refined look.

Make a Crosscut Jig

A crosscut jig is simply a piece of plywood with a bottom cleat that "hooks" onto the edge of a board, and a perpendicular top guide that's used as a saw guide. To build one, screw a 1x2 cleat to one edge of a scrap of plywood, flip it over, use a square to draw a line perpendicular to that cleat and screw another 1x2 to that line. Set your saw to 16 degrees, then run the table of your circular saw along the top cleat and cut off the edge of the plywood. TaDa! You've created a crosscut jig.

To use it, mark your board, align the cutting edge of the jig with the mark, snug the bottom cleat against the edge of the board, then turn on the saw and cut. Since the cuts are angled at 16 degrees, this jig can only be used to make 16-degree cuts. But you can see how easy it is to make one for non-angled cuts.

Once you make a jig, drill a hole in it and hang it on a nail. Also spray paint part of it yellow, so it doesn't mistakenly wind up in the scrap pile.

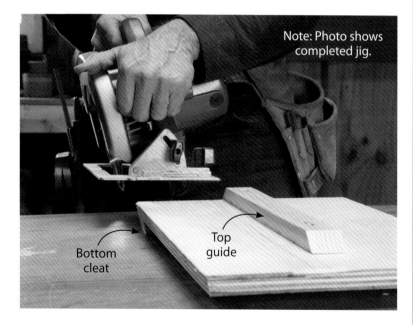

Note: Photo shows completed jig.

Bottom cleat

Top guide

Pyramid Bookshelf

A fastener-free bookshelf you can carry under one arm

It took the Egyptians over 20 years to build the Great Pyramid of Giza— and when they were done, they had a structure that could only do one thing: Hold the remains of one dead, conceited pharaoh. You can build this pyramid-shaped bookcase in a lot less time (hopefully) and put it to better use. Better yet, when it's time to move, you can disassemble the components, stack them flat and carry them away under one arm. Try doing that with a pyramid.

STUFF YOU'LL NEED	
1" x 3" x 6' oak	2
½" x 3' oak dowels	3
1" x 8" x 3', 4' or 5' oak	3

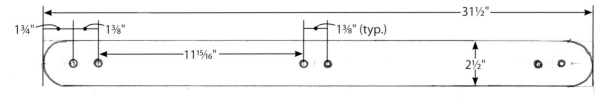

How to build it

Cut the four legs to length. Mark the positions of the dowels on one leg, then lay the three other legs next to it and use a square to transfer the marks across the other legs. Drill the dowel holes as shown in photo 1. If you have access to a drill press, use it. If you don't, use the simple little jig shown to help keep your bit square to the work surface. To build it, cut a 1x2 and piece of cove molding two inches long—the ends must be square—then glue them together. Position the tip of the drill bit on your mark, snug the jig against the bit, then use that to guide the bit.

Round the ends of the legs with a jigsaw, then sand them smooth. Cut twelve dowel segments 9-in. long. See the "bump jig" tip in the segment on power mitersaws (page 111) for a fast, accurate way to do this.

Use the serrated jaws of a pliers to create indentations or flutes (photo 2) on the dowel ends for the glue to nestle into. Apply glue, then tap six dowels into the holes of one leg, then position the other leg and tap that into place (photo 3). You want the ends of the dowels to be even with the sides of both legs, so keep flipping the legs over and tapping the dowel ends until they're flush. Give the legs one more sanding to remove glue and protruding dowel ends.

Make your shelves anywhere from 3 ft. to 5 ft. long. They can be the same length or shorter from bottom to top to reflect the angle of the legs. To set up your shelves, hold the legs vertically, slide the three shelves in between the dowel pairs, then spread the legs outward until friction "does its thing" and the unit feels solid.

1 Drill the dowel holes based on the measurements in the illustration. Use the jig to keep the bit square to the surface and use a backer board to minimize splintering.

2 Use the serrated jaws of a pliers to create grooves in the ends of the dowels. This will create room for the glue to nestle into.

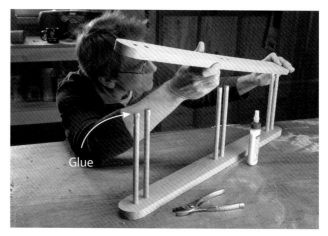

Glue

3 Assemble the ladder sides by tapping six dowels into one leg, then positioning the opposite leg and tapping it into place. You want the ends of the dowels to be even with the sides of the legs.

Organization & Charging Station
Get rid of countertop clutter—and get a charge out of it

Most countertops are cluttered enough—even before the cell phones, iPods, cameras and mail land on them in the evening. This organizer provides a convenient place for charging electrical doodads and sorting mail and papers. Better yet, the power strip concealed under the hinged lid eliminates the outlet shortage and dreaded "tangled cord syndrome" that plagues many families.

You can build your station any size or shape to accommodate the needs of your busy household. You can even construct yours so it hangs on the wall (though you'll need to hinge the lid differently).

STUFF YOU'LL NEED

1" x 10" x 6' pine	1
1" x 6" x 2' pine	1
1" x 4" x 3' pine	1
¾-in. cove molding	5 ft.
Piano hinge	18 inches

TIP ★ *Emergency Drill Bit*

If all your small drill bits have bitten the dust, make your own. Use a nipper or pliers to snip off the head of a finish nail, then chuck that into your drill. It'll be a little slower, but it'll do the job. Wear safety goggles when you snip—those little heads fly everywhere.

How to build it

Cut the two sides based on the dimensions in the illustration. Nail the bottom and midway shelves (ours are 18" long; yours can be longer or shorter) to the sides, then install the pigeon-hole partitions (photo 1). Cut notches in the 1x4 front panel, drill a large access hole near the 1x4 back panel, then nail these in place, making certain they're square to the top platform. Cut the top lid to size and secure it to the back panel with a piano hinge (photo 2). Use an awl to create starter holes for the tiny screws.

Install cove molding around the base (photo 3) and front edge of the top. You can nail a thin strip of wood along the tops of the side members to cover the end grain and along the front edge of the "charging platform" to prevent devices from falling or vibrating off. You can also upholster the platform with a piece of felt to create a softer resting place.

Place a multi-outlet power strip in the hinged box and snake the cord out through the hole in the back. Use the slots in the front panel for running the charger cords that connect your devices to the power strip. Designate a cubbyhole for each family member, then put your station to work.

1 Cut the pieces to length, then install the horizontal shelves and vertical cubbyhole dividers. Use glue and finish nails to secure the parts.

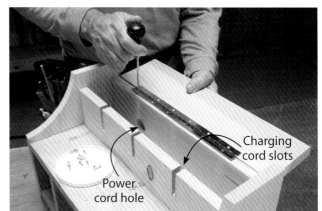

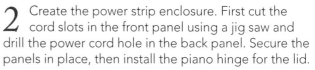

Charging cord slots

Power cord hole

2 Create the power strip enclosure. First cut the cord slots in the front panel using a jig saw and drill the power cord hole in the back panel. Secure the panels in place, then install the piano hinge for the lid.

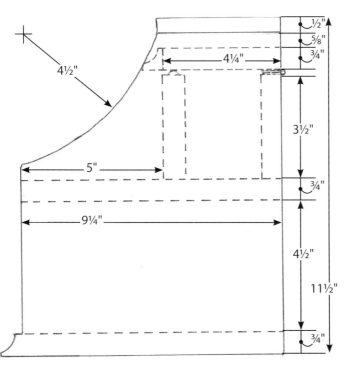

4½"

4¼"

½"
5⁄8"
¾"

5"

3½"

¾"

9¼"

4½"

11½"

¾"

3 Install cove molding around the base of the station, along the edge of the lid, and other places to cover end grain and add a decorative touch.

Cheatin' Corner Shelf
It's not unethical to build this way—just SMART!

Raise your hand if you—or someone in your family—have lots of doo-dads, thingamajigs and knick-knacks, but no place to put them. Wow, it's unanimous! This simple-to-build corner shelf unit puts underused corners to work by creating storage space for all that stuff.

We made the shelves by cutting a pine disc or "round," purchased at a home center for around $15, into quarters. Some might consider this cheating, but the store-bought round only cost a few bucks more than the wood you'd buy to make your own—and it was a lot less hassle. Plus, the disc is a full inch thick, has rounded edges, and is flat and smooth.

STUFF YOU'LL NEED

24-in. diameter pine round	1
1" x 2" x 40"	3
1" x 3" x 40"	1
¾" x ¾" square dowels	9 li. ft.

How to build it

Cut the shelves into quarters (photo 1), then sand the edges; it's easier to sand them now than after the shelf is assembled. Cut the legs to length, lay them side-by-side, then mark the shelf positions on all of the legs at the same time with the help of a square. We spaced our shelves 9 inches apart. When you build the L-shaped upright for the back corner, butt the 1x2 into the 1x3, so the legs of the "L" appear symmetrical. Select the best side of each slice and position it face-up as you build the shelf (photos 2 and 3). Use a square to periodically check that the shelves are square to the uprights as you work. If not, lightly rack the frame until it's square.

Make sure the horizontal 1x3 shelf backs (photo 4) fit tightly as you install them; they add rigidity to the shelf. Add ¾" x ¾" wood strips to the centers of the uprights to add extra support for the shelves and a decorative look. Feel free to use a different molding for a different look.

1 Divide a pre-cut pine "round" into four equal pie slices, then cut them using a circular saw. Sand the edges before assembling the shelf unit.

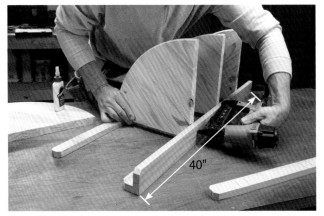

40"

2 Glue and nail the shelves to the layout marks on the uprights. The back upright consists of a 1x2 and 1x3 nailed to one another in an "L" shape.

3 Secure the third leg, then use a square to make sure the uprights are still square to the shelves. Let the glue dry before moving on to the next step.

Shelf back

4 Glue and nail the shelf backs in place. Cut them to fit tightly; they help take "the wiggle" out of the shelf unit. Add the ¾" x ¾" pieces to the uprights as shown in the lead photo and illustration.

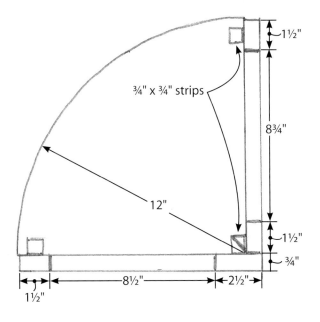

¾" x ¾" strips

1½"

8¾"

12"

1½"

¾"

8½" 2½"

1½"

TIP ★ *Tip Proofing*

If you have climbing cats or curious toddlers in the household, secure this shelf to the wall with a couple of long drywall screws to prevent tipping.

Jigsaw Puzzle Chairs

Five comfortable chairs from one sheet of plywood? You bet.

I call this the jigsaw puzzle chair for three reasons. First, the pieces are cut from the plywood like a big jigsaw puzzle. Second you can build the entire thing using only a jigsaw (though it's faster using a circular saw for the straight cuts). And third, when you tell people the chair is made from only a 2' x 3' sheet of plywood, they're puzzled how you could build such a clever thing. The fact is, this chair is so clever you can build five of them from a single 4 x 8-ft. sheet of ¾-in. plywood.

STUFF YOU'LL NEED

Per chair:
¾" x 2' x 3' plywood
2" drywall screws, glue

How to build it

Use the measurements in the illustration to mark out all the straight lines on a sheet of plywood (photo 1). Create the 1-in. radius on the corners using a compass or small jar. You can make all the cuts with a jigsaw, but a circular saw—preferably one with a fine-tooth, plywood-cutting blade to avoid splintered edges—will make the straight cuts faster (photo 2).

Smooth the edges by hand sanding or using a power sander. Use clamps to hold the side frames upright (photo 3), then position the seat so it overhangs each of the side frames by one inch. Secure the seat to the side frames using 2-in. drywall screws. Cut 10-degree angles on both ends of the 4" x 14" center "scrap," then screw that between the front legs to help wiggle-proof the chair. Finally, lay the chair flat, center the back on the uprights of the side frames and screw that into place (photo 4).

TIP ★ *Patterns Are Faster*

If you're going to make several chairs, mark and cut out the first chair accurately, then use one of the side frames as a pattern for tracing the parts for additional chairs.

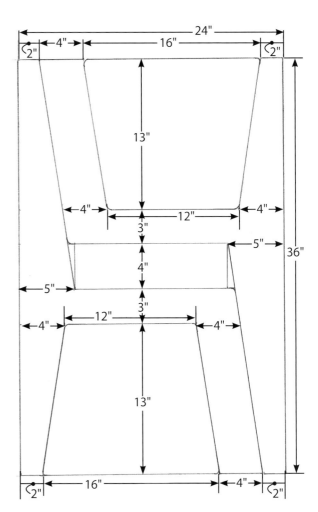

1 Mark out the chair parts. Use a drywall square or framing square to draw the four parallel lines that run "the short way" across the plywood. Then mark and draw the angled lines. Use an object with about a 1-inch radius to mark the small curves.

2 Cut out the components. Make plunge cuts (see the sidebar) with your circular saw to cut the inner lines, then use a jigsaw to finish up.

3 Using clamps to hold the legs upright, install the seat so it overhangs the side frames by one inch. Cut the short front brace to fit between the legs, then install it.

4 Center the back on the uprights and secure it with screws. Fill the screw holes with putty, sand, then apply a coat of primer and two coats of paint.

Making the Plunge

The secret to making accurate plunge cuts is to work decisively. Set the cutting depth to about ⅞-in., align the blade with your cut line, place the nose of the saw firmly on the plywood, then retract the blade guard. Turn on the saw, then slowly—but firmly—lower the spinning blade into the plywood and push the saw forward. If you approach this timidly, the saw can catch on the plywood and kick back toward you. Note, as you lower the blade, the initial plunge cut will be several inches long. Position your saw along the line so the initial plunge doesn't cut where you don't want it to cut. If you've never made a plunge cut, practice on scrap plywood until you get it right. If you still don't feel comfortable, use a jigsaw for all your cuts.

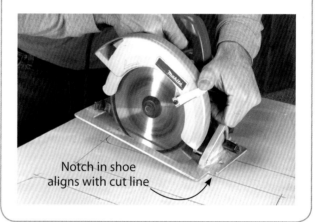

Notch in shoe aligns with cut line

Make it your own

- Less expensive plywood has a "good side" and a "bad side"; if you use that, you'll wind up with a chair that has one good side facing in and the other good side facing out—a scenario that would make Louis Vuitton roll over in his grave. We suggest you use plywood with two good sides.

- If you own a router, use a "round over" bit to soften the edges of the components before assembling the chairs.

- You can glue the components together for added strength, but if you're a nomad, use just the screws so the chair parts can be disassembled and stacked flat for the move.

Criss-Cross Plywood Table

Build this one-sheet wonder, knock it down, store it anywhere

If you're looking for a table that's easy to build, easy to store and easy on the budget, here's one for you. The three parts are cut from a single sheet of ½" x 4' x 8' plywood, and the table can easily be built in an afternoon. If you need to stash or move it, all you need to do is lift the top, "uncross" the legs and slip the pieces into the back of a closet. And Eureka! It's the perfect complement to the jigsaw puzzle chair in this book.

STUFF YOU'LL NEED	
½" x 4' x 8' plywood	1
¾" x 12" cove molding or wood strips	8

How to build it

Layout the three parts of the table on a 4' x 8' sheet of plywood. To draw the circular top, install a screw dead center on the plywood, hook the end of your tape on it, position your pencil on the 18-in. mark and use that as a gigantic compass. Next draw the legs; a large drywall square will help you work faster and more accurately. With the three main parts marked out, draw a pair of lines ½-in. apart through the center of the plywood (photo 1). Those lines will be the edges of the slots you cut in the legs so they can nest together, as well as the edges of the channels you nail on the top to hold those legs.

Use a jigsaw and circular saw to cut out the three parts (photo 2). Note, when you cut out the top, you automatically get the arched bottoms of the legs. Cut the slits in the legs so they can be fitted into one another when you assemble the table. The slit in one leg enters from the top, in the other from the bottom. Use the round top as a template for marking the curved sides of the legs (photo 3), then cut them out. Use glue and brads to install short pieces of cove molding or 1x2s to the bottom of the table (photo 4). Use a spacer that's a little over ½-in. wide to ensure the channels you create are wide enough for the legs to easily slip into.

To assemble the table, line up the slots in the legs and slide them together until the top edges are flush as shown in the background of photo 4. Then slip the legs into the channels (photo 5). When everything fits right, disassemble the table, sand the edges, prime and paint, then reassemble the table.

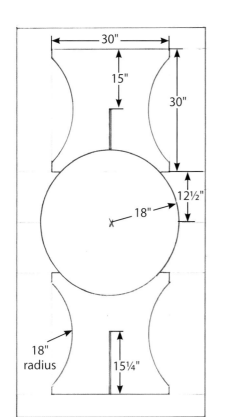

1 Use the measurements in the illustration to mark out the tabletop and legs. Drive a screw in the center of the sheet, then use a tape measure and pencil to mark the circumference of the top.

Make it your own

If you want to make your table stronger and more stable, construct it out of ¾-inch plywood. Or, after it's assembled, you can screw 2x2s into the corners where the legs intersect. This will add a few minutes to your assembly and disassembly times, but adds rigidity.

If you use hardwood plywood and want to leave the wood natural, you can apply pressure sensitive wood edging to cover the edges of the plywood. It's usually ¾ inches wide and available in oak, birch and maple. It can be purchased at most home centers or through woodworking specialty stores like Rockler or Woodcraft.

2 Use a jigsaw and circular saw to cut out the parts. Note that the slot in one leg enters from the top; in the other, from the bottom.

3 Clamp the legs together, then use the edge of the tabletop to mark the curved edges of the legs. Use a jigsaw to cut through both layers at the same time.

Spacer block

4 Glue and nail molding or wood strips to the bottom of the table to create channels for the legs to fit into. Use a scrap piece of plywood the same thickness as the legs to make sure the spacing is correct.

5 Test fit the legs in the slots, then flip the table over. Once you're sure everything fits, disassemble the three parts, sand the edges, then apply your finish of choice.

Maggie's Cookbook Stand

A splash-free stand for high-speed cooks

It's easy for me to find my daughter Maggie's favorite recipes. All I have to do is thumb though her cookbooks until I find the pages splattered with tomato sauce, egg yolk or UFI (Unidentified Flying Ingredients). A well-used cookbook is a sign of a passionate cook—but when it becomes difficult to tell whether the recipe calls for ½ tablespoon or ½ cup of sugar, it's time to take action.

This cookbook stand will keep your cookbooks and magazines up and off the counter, open to the right page, and at an angle that's easy to read. And if you're working off a recipe card, you can simply clip it to the shield with a binder clip. The dowel framework makes the rack lightweight and easy to clean—and the plexiglass windshield helps deflect flying artichokes.

We show it holding a magazine, but it really excels at holding cookbooks—it's just that when we put a book in the rack, it covered up everything for the photo!

How to build it

Cut the four pieces for the back frame to the dimensions shown in photo 2, then drill the ¾-in.-deep holes in the side members to accommodate the dowels (photo 1). Cut the dowels to length, insert them in the frame holes, then secure the corners of the frame together using nails and glue (photo 2).

Use a circular saw or table saw to cut a ⅟₁₆" groove in the top edge of the front bar to hold the plexiglass shield. We made a simple jig out of a few scraps of wood and a couple of clamps (photo 3). After cutting the groove, bore ½-in.-deep holes in the ends for the bar for the short dowels that allow it to pivot.

Cut out the two feet and drill the four holes in each—three for the long cookbook support dowels and one for the pivoting front bar. Remember, they're mirror images of one another. Insert 1-in.-long dowels in each end of the pivot bar and assemble the rack as shown in photo 4. Apply glue to the holes and to the feet where they connect to the upright frame. Use nails to secure the feet to the back frame. Make sure the feet are square to the back frame. Rotate the pivot bar a few times while the glue is drying to make sure excess glue doesn't prevent it from pivoting.

Apply a couple of coats of clear finish. Cut the plexiglass to size and slide it into the slot. Then get cooking!

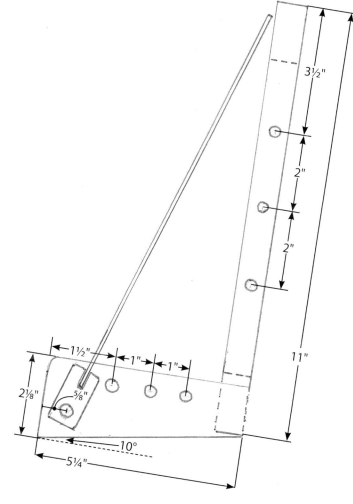

1 Drill ⅜"-diameter holes for the dowels in the two side members of the back frame. Use masking tape as a guide to drill consistent depth holes.

12" dowels

14"

11"

2 Assemble the back frame with the dowels in place. If you're hand nailing the corners together, predrill the holes; if you have a pneumatic brad nailer, use it.

Saw guide

14½" dowels

3 Use a circular saw or table saw to cut a groove in the front bar to hold the plexiglass. We made a simple jig using a 2x6 as a "bed" and a scrap piece of cove molding as a saw guide.

4 Drill the four holes in each of the feet and apply dabs of glue in each hole, plus on the base where it joins the back frame. Nail the feet to the back frame.

Plywood, Pharoahs and PT Boats

Plywood has been around a long time—so long in fact, that thinly shaved layers of wood, glued together like a sandwich, have been found in the tombs of Egyptian pharaohs. But it didn't catch on all that quickly; when it was introduced to the general public during the 1905 Portland World's Fair it was greeted with only a few stifled yawns.

Its popularity was eventually spurred by some rather sensationalist uses. In the 1930s, it was used to build a boat that endured a 600-mile trip down the raging Colorado River, and for the sleds and huts Admiral Byrd used on his South Pole expedition. During WWII it was put to work building reconnaissance gliders, the famed "Mosquito" combat plane and PT boats for the Navy. By the end of the war, production was pushing 2 billion square feet annually. Today over 16 billion square feet of plywood are manufactured each year; enough to build a plywood road 12-ft. wide all the way to the moon.

What does this have to do with building simple furniture? Absolutely nothing—but facts like this make you a brilliant conversationalist at parties.

Plywood is made of thin plies of wood that have been stacked atop one another with the grain oriented in alternating directions, then glued together under great pressure. For both strength and appearance there are almost always an odd number of plies, most commonly three and five. The result is a material that's stable, strong and amazingly versatile. It can be used for sheathing roofs, making kayaks, constructing cabinets and—of course—building Ridiculously Simple Furniture.

When you walk down the plywood aisle of your home center—the place we bought all the plywood used in this book, by the way—you'll be greeted by several dozen choices. But to select the right plywood there are only a few basic things you need to know:

- There are **hardwood** and **softwood** plywoods. The most commonly available hardwood plywoods have surface veneers of maple, oak and birch. These are most often used to build cabinets, furniture and other projects where you want the grain of the wood to show. Most softwood plywoods are made of pine, fir or larch, and are commonly—but surely not always—used for construction and remodeling.

- The **veneer faces** of plywood panels are graded A, B, C or D. "A" veneers have the fewest defects while D have the most. When you see plywood labeled A-B, it indicates one side is very good, and the other is pretty good. When you see plywood labeled C-D it means neither side looks that great; plywood like this is usually used for structural panels where appearance isn't important.

- Hardwood plywoods are made with a variety of **cores**, each with their own strengths and weaknesses. Lumber core plywood is expensive, but excels at holding screws and other fasteners. Particleboard core plywood is inexpensive, but lousy at holding fasteners. Multiply core has a solid uniform looking edge.

- **Medium density fiberboard (MDF)**, with its smooth, uniform surface, is relatively inexpensive and ideal for projects that will be painted. But there are drawbacks: It's heavy, swells and warps with excess moisture, and dulls blades quickly. And it raises such a fine dust that Bill, the photographer, grimaces and frowns whenever I cut it in his studio.

MDF
(medium density fiberboard)

CD
plywood

Oak plywood

Birch plywood

Router Fundamentals 101

A router can take an average-looking board or piece of furniture and turn it into something special in seconds. They can do lots of different things, but shine when it comes to rounding over the edges of a board or adding a decorative profile.

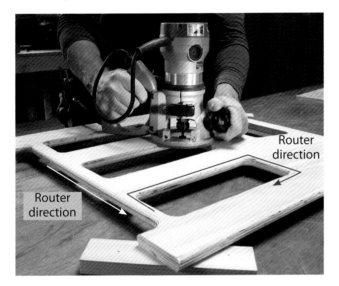

Move the Router So the Cutters Rotate into the Wood

Looking down onto your router, the bit rotates clockwise. Since you want the cutters to bite into the wood, move your router from left to right along the edge of a board facing you; move the router clockwise when routing the inside of a cutout.

A Few Basics

- **Several shallow passes** are better than one deep one. When you're cutting a deep profile, don't try to do it all in one shot; you're more likely to splinter and burn the edges of your work piece. And it can take its toll on your bit, your router and maybe even you. Instead make two or three progressively deeper passes until you reach the proper depth.

- **Route the end grain first**, then the edges. The end grain of a board is more likely to splinter or chip, especially at the corner. To help "clean up" the damage, rout the end grain first, then the edges. Your edge pass will help remove any splinters.

- **Buy bits with roller bearings**, not "nibs." Edge bits always have a guide that rides along the edge of the board while the cutters above do their thing. Some guides consist simply of a "nib" built right into the bit that spins along with the bit. These bits are inexpensive, but much more likely to burn the wood, or sometimes even dig into it and wreck it. Bits with roller bearings are more expensive, but do a much (much) better job. They don't spin with the bit, and create a smoother, cleaner profile.

Clamp Down Small Boards

Router bits have enough oomph to kick a board right off your workbench. Clamp a board down—even if it means repositioning it a few times. On thin pieces of wood, raise the board up so the bit doesn't contact the work surface.

Wine Bottle Quartet
A quartet of simple wine racks for storing, displaying & giving

Think of the next four projects not so much as furniture for people, but as "furniture for wine." After all, even a bottle of vino needs a comfortable place to sit while waiting for the cork to be popped. All four projects are simple to build and cost way less than a bottle of Chateau Lafite. They're perfect for using up scrap pieces of lumber from other projects; in fact, the Triple Bottle wine rack is made almost entirely from scraps from the Crescent Moon rack.

They also make unique gifts; rather than presenting your host or hostess a hum-ho bottle of wine, you can present him or her with a useful, handmade conversation piece to go with it as well.

Houdini Bottle Holder

A gravity-defying conversation piece

A project can't get much simpler—or more gravity defying—than this: Cut an angle on one end of a board, cut a curve on the other, drill a hole, and you're done. To make the board "balance," slide the neck of the bottle in and out of the hole, until the board stands on its own; it will work with standard-size wine bottles.

A good bump, nudge or vibration can send the board and bottle toppling—so after showing off your Houdini-like talents to your date or dinner guests, we suggest you lay the board flat and use it as a serving tray.

STUFF YOU'LL NEED

1" x 6" x 12" board	1

How to build it

Cut the end of a board at a 33-degree angle, using a square to help guide your circular saw or jigsaw. Cut the board to its final length, then shape the top. Bore the bottle neck hole, using a 1¼-in. spade bit. Use a backer board so you don't splinter the back of the board when the bit bursts through. Sand the board smooth, then rout the edges if you wish.

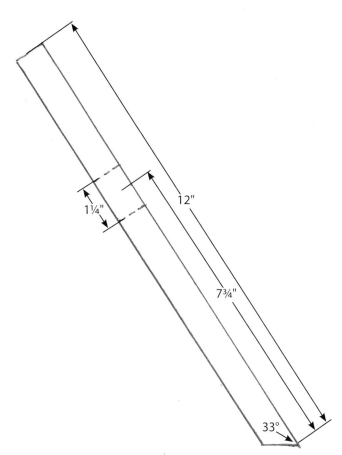

1¼"

12"

7¾"

33°

1 Cut a 33-degree angle on the end of a 12-in.-long 1x6. Use a speed square to help guide the table of your saw to create a straight cut.

TIP ★ *Belt Sander Candor*

If you're shopping for a belt sander, consider buying a "flat top" version. You can use it upside down for sanding small and irregularly-shaped parts.

2 Bore a 1¼-in. hole. Round the top of your holder on the sander and use a router to round over the edges if you wish.

Crescent Moon Bottle Rack

A creative way to cradle your wine

This wine cradle was inspired by one my wife and I saw while traipsing through the vineyards of Sonoma County. It's made from a maple board sandwiched between two oak boards—you can make yours out of any type wood you want (or have lying around in your scrap pile). Save your cutouts; you can use them to build the triple bottle wine rack shown later in this section.

> ### STUFF YOU'LL NEED
>
> 1" x 6" x 12" oak
> or other hardwood   3

How to build it

Trace around the bottom of a 5-gallon drywall bucket twice to establish the crescent moon shape (photo 1). If you're bucketless, the diameter is 10½ in. Use a jigsaw to cut out the shape, then use that as a template to trace your crescent moon shape onto two more boards. Cut them out.

Glue and clamp the three pieces together (photo 2). The edges won't align exactly, just line them up as well as you can. Let the glue dry overnight before cutting the 1⅛-in. bottleneck hole. Use the cutouts as backer boards (photo 3); the wood will be less likely to splinter when the bit breaks through the far side.

Use a belt sander or other power sander to smooth the inside and outside surfaces. You can do it by hand, but it will take you a while if your rack is made of hardwood. Apply several coats of Danish oil or other clear finish. Make sure the finish coats the inside of the bottleneck hole.

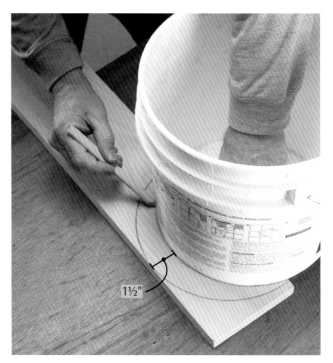

1 Trace around the base of a drywall bucket to draw the outer curve, then move the bucket 1½ in. and trace the inner curve. Use a jigsaw to cut out the crescent shape. Use that board as a pattern for the other two.

2 Glue and clamp the three pieces together. Unless you're a jigsaw genius, chances are the three pieces won't line up perfectly; just align the edges as closely as you can to minimize the amount of sanding.

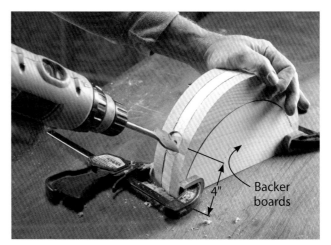

3 Drill the 1⅛-in. hole for the bottle neck. Use the three cutout scraps as backing material to minimize splintering when the bit breaks through the opposite side. Use a belt sander to smooth the inner and outer surfaces.

Triple Bottle Cradle

Use "leftovers" to create this simple rack

We hope you hung onto the semi-circular cutouts left over from the Crescent Moon bottle rack—because all you need are those scraps and a dowel to create this project.

You can print out a full size pattern of the front and back cradle parts by visiting www.ridiculouslysimpleprojects.com. Use carbon paper to transfer the patterns directly onto your wood.

STUFF YOU'LL NEED

1" x 6" x 10"	2
(or cutouts from Crescent Moon project)	
½" x 8" dowels	2

On the web

Download and print out a full size pattern of the triple wine rack at www.ridiculouslysimplefurniture.com, then use carbon paper to transfer the pattern directly onto your wood.

How to build it

Transfer the measurements from the illustration onto your semi-circular wood cutouts (Note: the single illustration below contains cutout patterns for both pieces). If you didn't save the cutouts from the Crescent Moon project, cut two semicircles with 5¼-in. radii. Clamp the pieces firmly to your work surface as you cut, and work carefully so you don't damage the narrow "ears" that separate the wine bottles.

It's easiest to sand the cradles before assembling the piece. You can round over the edges with a router bit if you want a softer look.

Make certain to drill the ½-in. holes for the dowels straight and true. The dowels and dowel connection are what create rigidity and a solid joint. Drill the hole with a ¹⁵⁄₃₂-in. bit to assure a snug fit. Stain the completed piece if you wish, then apply two coats of a clear finish.

1 Transfer the measurements from the illustration onto the semicircular cutouts from the Crescent Moon Rack. Use a thin, fine-tooth blade to make the tight turns and leave a clean cut.

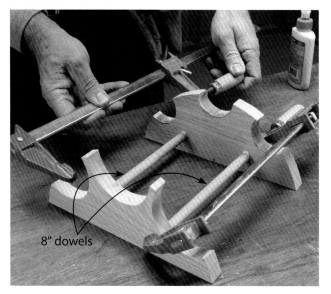

8" dowels

2 Bore two ¹⁵⁄₃₂-in.-diameter holes ½ in. deep. Apply glue to the dowel ends, insert them in the holes, and clamp the rack together. Use an angle square to make certain the dowels are square to the end pieces, and that the end pieces are square to the work surface.

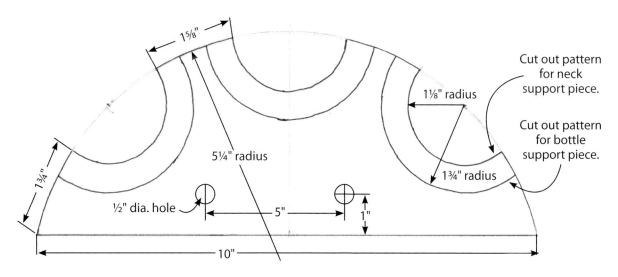

1⅝"

5¼" radius

1¾"

½" dia. hole

5"

1"

1⅛" radius

Cut out pattern for neck support piece.

Cut out pattern for bottle support piece.

1¾" radius

10"

Wine for Two

Your very own tabletop butler

Here's another clever project/gift/conversation piece for wine lovers and wine givers. It's simply an oval-shaped piece of ½-in.-thick wood with three holes and two slots cut into it. It's another great way to use leftover wood—and it's a darn fine gift you can make in less than an hour.

You can modify the basic concept by creating a "yoke" that will accommodate three, four or more glasses; I've seen round, square and propeller-shaped versions.

STUFF YOU'LL NEED

½" x 6" x 12"	1

How to build it

Use the half-pattern illustration as a guide for drawing the shape of the bottle yoke and the position of the holes on your wood. You can print out a full size pattern by visiting www.ridiculouslysimplefurniture.com. Use a 1¼-in. or 1⅛-in. spade bit to drill the hole for the bottle neck and a ¾-in. bit for the wine glass stems (photo 1). Make sure to clamp it down! Spade bits have a tendency to bite into unclamped boards

and spin them around like a helicopter blade. It can hurt.

Use a jigsaw or coping saw to cut the curved slots, then rout the edges. Make the slots wide enough to accommodate the stems of your glasses. You'll need to use sandpaper to chamfer the edges of the narrow wine stem slots since your router bit won't fit. Hand sand all the other surfaces until smooth, then apply a finish.

1 Transfer the shape of the yoke and the position of the holes from the illustration to your board. Use a backer board when you drill so the bit doesn't splinter the wood as it exits the other side. Cut the two wine glass stem slots with a jigsaw.

2 Use a chamfer bit to shape both sides of the yoke. Raise the board off the work surface and clamp it down; otherwise the guide bearing on the bit will hit the work surface.

On the web

Download and print out a full size half-pattern of this project at www.ridiculouslysimplefurniture.com, then use carbon paper to transfer the pattern directly onto your wood.

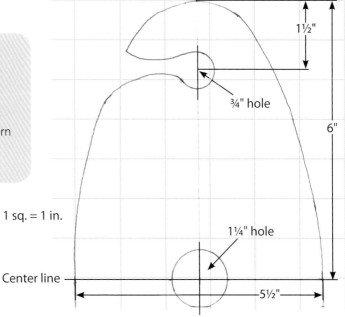

1 sq. = 1 in.

1½"

¾" hole

6"

1¼" hole

Center line

5½"

Kitchen Cart

A kitchen addition on wheels— made from stair spindles and 1x4s

Need more elbow room in the kitchen, but no place to put those elbows? Build this roll-around kitchen cart. It has plenty of space on top for chopping and mixing, and plenty of space below for stashing large items like mixing bowls and platters. The handle gives you a place to hang a towel or two and if you really want to make full use of your new kitchen addition, install cup hooks on the stretchers and hang utensils and pans.

STUFF YOU'LL NEED

1¾" x 1¾" x 32" stair spindles	4
1" x 4" clear pine	36'
18" x 36" pine or maple panel	1
1-in. dowel	2'
1 x 2 scraps for securing top	6 pcs.

Casters, white glue, finish nails

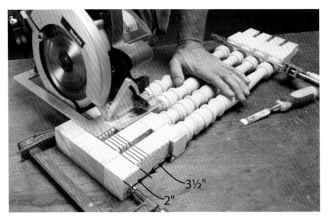

1 Cut the spindles to length, clamp them together, then mark the location of the top and bottom stretchers. Cut a series of ⅜-in.-deep cuts, spaced about ½ inch apart, with your circular saw on two adjacent sides of each spindle.

2 Use a chisel to remove the nibs. Hold the chisel at one end of the notch, then pry toward the center to snap off the nibs; repeat at the other end. Then smooth the surfaces with your chisel held horizontally.

How to build it

Cut the spindles to length, then notch them as shown in photo 1. Creating notches for the stretchers—rather than just nailing them to the sides of the spindles—adds strength and rigidity to the cart; important since the cart will be moved around more than most pieces of furniture.

Clamp the spindles together and notch them all at the same time so they'll all be the same width (preferably the CORRECT width, which is 3½-in.) Once you've removed the waste (photo 2), smooth

TIP ★ *Paint Before Assembling*

If your cart is going to have a painted frame and a natural top, apply the finishes separately before joining the two together. If you plan on using your island as a cutting board, install a butcherblock maple top instead of a pine one. They're more expensive, but more durable.

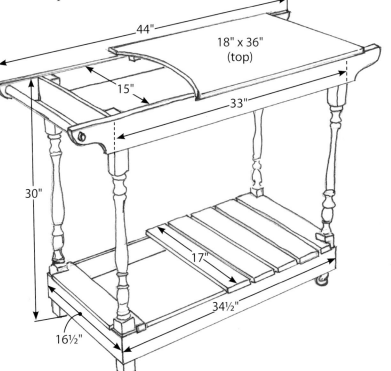

the notches with your chisel held flat. It's okay if the notches aren't perfectly flat; the top and bottom stretchers will cover them.

When you install the stretchers, do it in this order: Install the short upper stretcher between two legs, then, making sure the legs are equally spaced, install the short mitered bottom stretcher to create each leg assembly. Place these two leg assemblies on your workbench and install the two long bottom stretchers (photo 3). Last, install the two long top stretchers (photo 4) that extend past the spindles to create the cart's handles.

Cut the top to size and secure it to the top frame (photo 5), then cut the bottom slats and nail them in place (photo 6). Drill holes and install a 1-in. dowel through the handles on one side of the cart; you can do this on both sides (or neither side) if you prefer.

We installed just two casters, that way the cart could be easily wheeled around, but remain stationary when in use. You can install two, four or no casters, depending on how you intend to use the cart. If you use four casters, install ones that lock. You'll need to adjust the lengths of the legs to accommodate your casters. We cut two shorter to accommodate the casters, then added short blocks to the other two to even things out.

3 Cut and install the stretchers, nestling them into the notches and securing them with glue and finish nails. Use a large square (or check by cross taping) to make sure the frame remains square.

4 When installing the long top stretchers, measure to make sure the spacing between the leg units and the overhang extending beyond the legs are equal.

5 Position the completed framework on the top, making sure it's centered. Glue and nail 1x2 scraps to the cart to connect the top to the frame.

6 Cut the bottom slats to length, then notch the two ends slats to fit around the legs. Position the other slats so they're equally spaced, then glue and nail them to the bottom stretchers.

Spice Drawer Organizer
A simple project for simplifying life

Searching for a special space for savory spices? (Say that three times real fast!) Well, if you've got an extra drawer you've got just the place. This insert holds your spices at a slight angle so they're easy to organize, locate and grab.

Measure the width of your drawer and make the insert ¼-in. narrower. If your drawer is long enough, you may be able to fit in a fourth tier. Keep flipping the insert over as you work so you can drive the brads through the ½-inch boards into the ¾-in. square dowels. Apply two coats of high gloss paint or clear finish so the surface is easy to keep clean.

STUFF YOU'LL NEED
¾" x ¾" square risers
½" x 6" boards

1 Use glue and one-inch brads to secure the ½" x 6" boards to the ¾" square risers.

Skinny Tower of Pizza

It spins, it stores, it frees up tabletop space

The pizza's coming—time to break out the plates, peppers, Parmesan and potato chips. Now the problem is, where do you put the pizza? The solution for clearing the clutter and creating more space is this pizza tower. It elevates the pizza to create more room on the table. It also incorporates a lazy Susan so it's easier to "pass the pizza," and has space on the base for stashing condiments. You'll find other uses for it too—like passing appetizers and rotating your Scrabble board.

The project is made all the easier by using an inexpensive lazy Susan turntable and a circular "clock face" disc purchased at a craft store. When it comes to using your stand, cut your pizza before placing it on the disc; otherwise you could create a leaning—or toppled—tower of pizza.

How to build it

Cut the two top and bottom members of the tower, then, after drawing diagonals from corner to corner, "bob" the corners at 45 degrees. Drill ½-in.-dia. holes, ½ in. deep at the corners (photo 1). Use masking tape as a depth guide and space all the holes equal distances from the corners.

The trick to mounting a lazy Susan is drilling the access hole you use for securing the lazy Susan to the disc after it's been secured to the top member. Temporarily center the disc on the top member of the tower, then mark and bore a ¾-in. access hole. Once that's done, secure the hardware to the top member of the tower (photo 2).

Draw an "X" on the back of your disc. Flip the top member upside down, then, sighting through the access hole, position the four screw holes of the lazy Susan hardware equally on the legs of the "X." Use

the access hole to install the screws (photo 3). Apply glue to both ends of four ½-in. dowels and insert them in the mounting holes. Use a square to make certain the dowels are square to the top and bottom tower members. Set a few bricks on the unit to keep the dowels pressed solidly in the holes until the glue dries. Sand, apply a protective finish, and you're done.

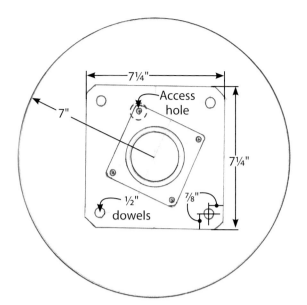

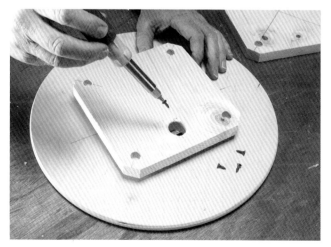

1 Cut the base pieces to size, then round or bob the corners. Drill ½-in. holes, ½ in. deep, equal distances from the corners on both pieces.

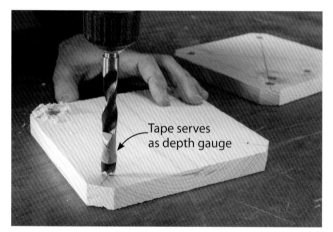

3 Mount the lazy Susan to the disc by driving in the screws via the access hole. Make certain the lazy Susan hardware is centered on the disc.

2 Drill the ¾-in.-dia. access hole that you'll use in the next step. Screw the corners of the lazy Susan to the top member of the tower.

4 Glue the four dowels in both sets of mounting holes. Use a square to make sure the dowels are square to the base pieces. Use bricks as "clamps" to hold the pieces together until the glue dries.

Aldo Leopold Bench

6 boards and 60 minutes create this comfy outdoor seat

If you're a beginning furniture maker, you'll be hard pressed to find a project simpler than this. With six pieces of wood, nine cuts and twenty screws you can create a bench that's not only surprisingly easy to build, but surprisingly easy to sit on as well.

There are a few keys to this simplicity. Most of the cuts are the same 30-degree angle. Many of the parts do double duty—the back legs serve as the seat supports and the front legs serve as the backrest support. And the seat is made from a pre-cut stair tread, with the front already rounded over for you.

STUFF YOU'LL NEED

2" x 8" x10' treated board	1
2" x 6" x 39" treated board	1
2" x 12" x 36" treated stair tread	1

How to build it

Cut your 2x8 to the lengths and angles shown in the illustration. As you mark the board (photo 1) you'll notice, since all the angles are the same, you get some "free" cuts; the angled end of one board is the angled start of another.

Screw the front and back legs to one another, using a scrap 2x4 to align the bottoms (photo 2). Make certain the legs in both assemblies are the same distance apart and that you build the assemblies as mirror images of one another. Position the leg assemblies upright, position the seat on top of the short legs, then secure it with drywall screws. We used a stair tread, but you can make your own out of a standard 2" x 12" if you wish. Finally, secure the 2x6 back in place (photo 3).

If you want to make the seat even sturdier, use exterior construction adhesive when securing the parts to one another.

1 Mark the lengths and 30-degree angles on the 2x8 as shown, then cut with a circular saw. If you wish, cut the additional little angles on the ends of the long pieces where the backrest will be attached (see next photo).

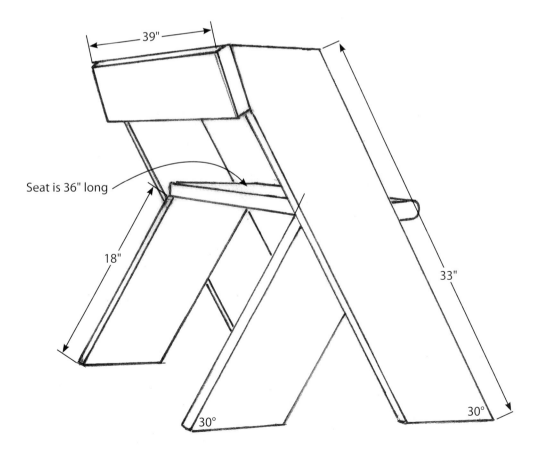

39"

Seat is 36" long

18"

33"

30°

30°

Cut to adjust
backrest angle

2 Assemble the legs, making sure you build them as mirror images of one another and that the legs are the same distance apart. Secure them with 2½-in. galvanized drywall screws.

Aldo Leopold in Boma'langombe

If lack of tools and experience are keeping you from building furniture, perhaps these students will inspire you. With only a dull handsaw, some rough lumber, a hammer and an urge to learn something new, these women students from Boma'langombe Secondary School in Tanzania built these two benches in less than two hours.

Work was nothing new for these six. For years they'd risen at 5:30 to haul firewood to boil the water—that they'd also hauled—for cooking breakfast. They studied by candlelight because there was no electricity. Two benches may not seem like a gigantic accomplishment, but—in a culture where women normally haul water, not swing a hammer—it is. Educate a boy in carpentry and you educate an individual. Educate a girl in carpentry and you educate a village.

Stair tread

3 Attach the seat by driving screws down through the seat into the tops of the legs and in from the sides. Then, make sure the bench is standing vertically and screw on the back.

Make it your own

The bench is most comfortable to sit on when your feet are resting on the ground. If you're vertically challenged, lop 2 or 3 inches off each leg.

- You can change the angle of the top 5½ in. of the long 2x8s to change the angle of the back. That's what we did. You may find a more vertical backrest more comfortable.

- You can make the bench longer by installing a longer seat and back (though a seat longer than 4 feet will start feeling bouncy).

- If you have a router, you can "soften" the edges of the bench with a roundover bit. Or use a jigsaw to arch the top of the backrest.

Sorting Out Angles

The way angles are denoted in books and on tools can be confounding. For instance, when you look at the photo below, you'll notice that the angle drawn on the right of the board could be designated as 30 degrees, 60 degrees or 120 degrees, depending on which way you look at it. Generally the angles you see on tool gauges and illustrations refer to how many degrees are being removed *from the square end of a board.* If in doubt, pause, look carefully at the diagram and the tool and ask yourself, "If I cut this board at this angle, are the pieces going to fit together right?" If still in doubt, cut a test piece.

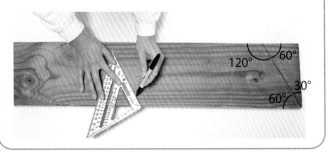

Portable Outdoor Chair
A simple seat for those on the go

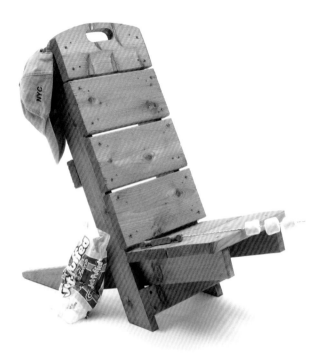

If your family needs comfy chairs for camping, sitting around the campfire, trips to the beach or just lazing around the backyard, look no further. If you're looking for chairs that are easy to stow and haul, you've found those, too. These portable outdoor chairs are great for kids, but surprisingly comfortable for adults to sit in, too.

This mini-Adirondack chair requires only basic tools and skills, a few hours and some radius edge deck boards. As long as you have the tools out why not make one for everyone in the family?

Stuff You'll Need

1" x 6" x 8' radius edge deck board	2

How to build it

Use a circular saw (photo 1) to rip one of the 6-in. deck boards in half, with one side being about ¼-in. wider than the other. Cut these to the lengths and angles shown in the illustration. Screw the 1x3 braces to the long backrest struts (photo 2). Make sure the space between the back struts is 10¼ inches, so the seat can slide in between for storage. Use galvanized screws to secure the seat slats and back slats to the backrest and seat struts. Curve the top of the uppermost back slat and cut in a handle for easy carrying.

Test fit the chair in both the "seated" and "stored" positions, then lightly sand all the parts to remove splinters and sharp edges. Apply two coats of exterior stain or a clear finish.

Safety Note: Be careful when getting into or out of the chair; it can teeter-totter on its front legs if you sit too far forward on the seat. You could squish your marshmallows—or worse.

1 Use a straight 1x2 as a saw guide or use a table saw to rip radius edge deck boards into two slightly unequal halves; make one side around 2⅞ in., the other around 2⅝ in.

2 To create the backrest, cut the 2⅞-in.-wide boards to the shape and dimensions shown in the illustration, then glue and screw the three cross braces in place.

3 Install the back slats and seat slats. Follow the dimensions shown in the illustration; otherwise you may not be able to slide the seat assembly into the back assembly for storage and toting.

TIP ★ *Avoid Rust and Stains*

Always use galvanized or coated nails and screws for outdoor projects. They'll last longer and won't rust and bleed all over your pretty project like standard fasteners will.

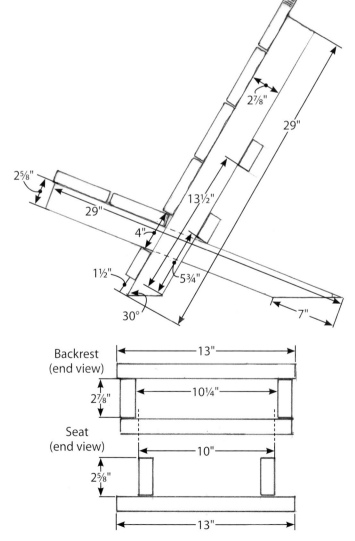

Measuring and Marking Tips

You've probably heard the saying "I've cut it twice and it's still too short." Usually the problem isn't how the board was cut, but how it was measured. With some projects—like picnic tables or outdoor planters—getting the measurements *exactly* right isn't critical. But with others it makes the difference between a project that looks well made and one that looks bush league.

To minimize measuring errors, try these tricks:

- Keep a piece of masking tape stuck to your tape measure for writing down measurements. Sometimes, by the time you cross the room, that $15\frac{7}{8}$-in. measurement has become a $17\frac{5}{8}$-in. measurement.

- Cut the longest pieces first. That way if you mismeasure or miscut a board, you can still use it for the shorter piece.

- Remember: There are no mistakes, only design opportunities. Sometimes it doesn't really matter if you cut something too short, just keep an eye out how that might affect other parts of the project.

Cut It the Right Length

Cutting on the wrong side of the line can create a board that's $\frac{1}{8}$-inch longer or shorter than the desired length. Always determine which side of the line you want to cut on before pulling the trigger.

Mark It with a "V" for Accuracy

When marking a board, indicate the exact measurement you want with the tip of a "V". It will minimize errors when cutting or positioning things.

Burn an Inch

When measuring from the short side of a miter, it's difficult to position the end of your tape in the exact right spot. Instead, position the "1-inch" mark of your tape on the miter, then add an inch to your desired measurement.

Mark, Don't Measure

When possible, position a board or molding and mark it in place instead of measuring. It's faster, more accurate and eliminates mental errors.

Crosstape to Assure Squareness

When the thing you build isn't square, funny things happen: Doors don't fit, drawers don't close, mitered corners don't meet and legs don't sit on the floor. To check a rectangle for squareness, measure the diagonals in both directions, then adjust the box until the measurements are equal. Then install a brace or back to keep it square.

Going in Circles

Most of us learned to use a compass in geometry class. I used mine mostly for poking holes in my tests and desk, but I eventually learned to draw a perfect circle—during detention. But what if you need to create a really large circle or lots of small curves?

In many cases you can simply trace around something at hand (first photo). Head to your kitchen and you'll find 1-in.-diameter shot glasses, 15-in.-diameter mixing bowls and everything in between. The coins in your pocket, paint cans in your basement and washers in your toolbox work well, too.

For larger circles all you need are a drywall screw, tape measure and pencil (second photo). Drive in the screw at the center point, hook the end of your tape over the screwhead, place your pencil firmly next to the measurement on the tape that corresponds to the radius and swing your curve.

Herb Bench

Parsley, sage, rosemary and thyme on your doorstep

My wife loves to walk out the door, snip off a few sprigs of fresh basil or parsley, then throw them in the pot of whatever she's cooking. She loves this little herb bench, too. She can grow the spices in pots right on our deck, and she can pick them without bending over. Better yet, spices look nice in the flowerpot and taste good in the cooking pot.

We built our herb bench from one-inch-thick cedar boards usually used for decking. Another cool feature is that the half-moon cutouts don't go into the scrap heap; they go into reinforcing and decorating the bench. Make sure to buy your pots before you build the bench. Pot sizes vary and you want to make sure the rim of the pot rests on the edge of the hole.

STUFF YOU'LL NEED
5/4" x 6" x 6' radius edge decking	2

How to build it

Measure your pots, then size the cutouts in the top boards so the rim of the pot will rest on the board (photo 1). Mark the pot cutouts, then separate the boards and use a jigsaw to cut out the six semi-circles. Be careful—you'll use these cutouts later on.

Cut the legs to length, position them in pairs, then draw the same diameter circle on the bottoms and cut them out (photo 2). Cut four cleats out of scrap material and use them to secure each pair of legs together. Make sure the cleats are the correct length and centered on the legs; they'll determine the position of the quarter-circle braces you install later. Flip the leg assembly over and screw a half-moon cutout to the other side (photo 3).

Place the two top boards on the work surface, position the leg assemblies on top and screw the cleats to the top boards. Next take two of the half-moons and cut them in half to create quarter circles. Install these quarter circles to serve as braces where the legs meet the top (photo 4).

Apply an exterior finish, then get planting and snipping!

1 Cut the two top boards to length—we made ours 40 in. long— clamp them together, then use a compass to mark the cutouts. Clamp, mark and cut the two leg units, too.

TIP ★ *Create More Space*

Install an extra board—supported by the two lower leg cleats—to create a lower shelf for seedling trays, hand tools and other potted spice plants.

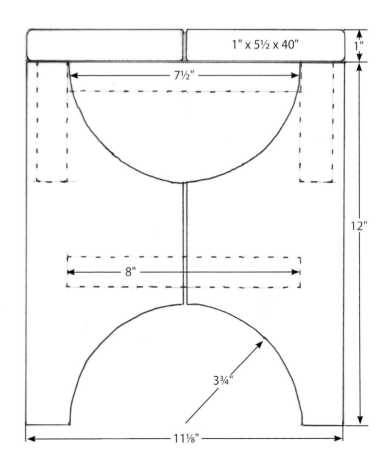

2 Use a jigsaw to cut out the semi-circles in the top boards and legs. Make sure to save the scraps.

3 Attach the two halves of the legs to one another with cleats, using 16d nails for spacers. Attach a half-moon scrap to the outside of each leg. Secure the legs to the top by driving screws through the cleats and into the top boards.

Cleats

4 Use the four cutouts from the bottoms of the legs for the corner braces. Predrill holes to minimize the chance of splitting.

Simple Patio Planter
An "L" of an easy planter to build

There are some pretty cool-looking concrete and pottery planters out there; we used to own one shaped like a pig. But sometimes the price just makes you want to squeal. Plus they're heavy to move around and can freeze and crack if you don't protect them over the winter. Here's a planter that'll make you as happy as a pig in the mud; it's attractive, easy to build and easy to modify to accommodate your needs.

The L-shaped legs take time to create, but they serve triple duty: They're the framework for attaching the sides, they're the legs for elevating the planter and they cover the edges of the plywood to give the corners a cleaner look. The sides are made from treated plywood and the finials are screw-on fence post caps you can purchase at most home centers.

STUFF YOU'LL NEED

4" x 4" x 6' (cedar or treated)	1
2" x 4" x 6' (cedar or treated)	1
2" x 2" x 3' (cedar or treated)	1
½" x 2' x 4' treated plywood	1
Post finials	4
Landscape plastic to line planter	

How to build it

Cut the legs to length. Set your circular saw to a depth of 2 inches and make cuts on two adjacent sides of each leg (photo 1). You want to remove a 2-in. x 2-in. portion of the leg so each side of the remaining "L" is 1½ inches wide.

Cut the treated plywood sides to size; the size will determine the overall length and width of your planter as well as how far off the ground the planter bottom will sit. Use galvanized screws and outdoor construction adhesive to secure the plywood to the backs of the legs (photo 2).

Use the 2 x 2-in. cutouts from the legs as cleats for holding the plywood bottom in place (photo 3). Cut a piece of plywood to fit in the bottom, drill drainage holes, then rest it on the cleats.

Cut short lengths of 2x2 (actual dimension, 1½" x 1½") wood and secure them between the legs at the bottom edge of the plywood to create a cleaner look. Cut and install the mitered 2x4s that frame the top. Use 3-in. galvanized screws to secure these pieces to the legs and to one another at the corners (photo 4). Drill holes for the finials, then screw them in place on each corner (photo 5).

We applied two coats of semi-transparent exterior stain. For variety, consider painting the finials a contrasting color before installing them.

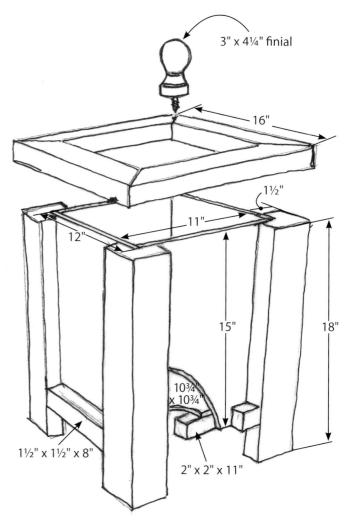

1 Set your circular saw to a depth of 2 inches and make intersecting cuts on adjacent sides of the leg to remove a 2 x 2 in. chunk. Screw a scrap block to your work surface to hold the leg in place while sawing.

2 Install the plywood sides using exterior construction adhesive and galvanized screws or nails. Note: To make the planter square, the last two pieces of plywood installed need to be 1 in. narrower than the first two.

3 Use the leg cutouts as cleats for holding the bottom piece of plywood in place. After those are installed, add the short 2x2 trim pieces between the legs at the bottom.

Leg cutout scraps

Fence post finials

5 Predrill holes and screw the finials in place. Apply the exterior finish of your choice. Drill a few drainage holes in the plywood bottom and drop it in place so it rests on the cleats. Line your planter with landscape plastic to help waterproof the inside. Add dirt, plants and enjoy.

4 Cut the top trim pieces so they overhang the legs by about ½ in., then screw them to the planter top. Pull the mitered corners tightly together by driving screws in through the sides.

Bonsai Plant Stand

An oriental-inspired stand you can use indoors or out

You can use this plant stand inside or outside; for Bonsai plants or Boston Ferns; on the deck or in the backyard. Like all good bonsai stands, it's designed to be attractive, yet not distract from the beauty of the plants displayed on it. We chose to make ours out of cedar because of its beauty, stability and rot resistance. You can build yours of treated wood if you plan to stain it or want to save a few dollars. It's easy to modify the basic design to make your stand larger, smaller, taller or shorter.

STUFF YOU'LL NEED

2" x 2" x 3' cedar	8
2" x 6" x 5' cedar	1

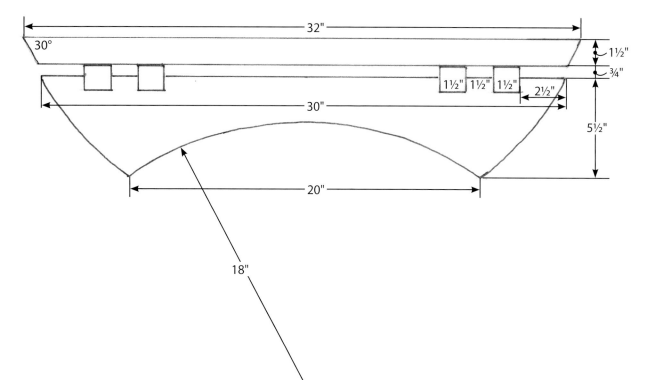

How to build it

Cut the legs to length, then draw the bottom arcs (photo 1). Since we needed to swing a large arc, we set a board perpendicular to the leg, drove a screw in and used that as the center point. Use a jigsaw to cut the arc and slightly curve the ends, then smooth the curves with a belt sander or by hand. Cut the notches that will hold the crosspieces in the legs with a jigsaw, then use a chisel to square off the bottoms of the notches (photo 2).

Cut the four 19½" crosspieces to the length and angle shown, lay them side by side and draw lines across them at 1½-in. intervals (photo 3). Tap them into the notches so they overhang the sides of the legs by about 1½ in. and screw them to the legs. Position the top slats on the crosspiece layout marks and secure them with 2¼-in. galvanized screws (photo 4). Apply a clear finish or stain, or leave the wood natural and let it turn a silvery gray.

1 Draw the arcs for the bottoms of the legs using a tape measure for a compass. Cut out the curve, then position the cutout and trace along the curved edge to establish the curved ends.

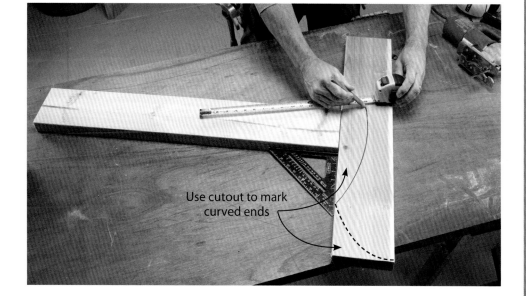

Use cutout to mark curved ends

2 Use a jigsaw to cut the sides of the notches and a chisel to square off the
bottom and remove the waste.

30° angle

3 Cut the four 19½" crosspieces to length, position
them side by side, then make layout marks at 1½
in. intervals.

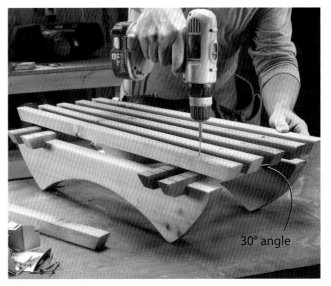

30° angle

4 Position the cross pieces in the notches, then
secure the top slats to them using galvanized
screws. If you want to take apart the stand for winter
storage, make sure you can get at the screws that
secure the crosspieces to the legs.

Mitersaw Heaven

There are two larger-than-a-breadbox power tools that will make your furniture building endeavors immensely—IMMENSELY—more enjoyable. One is the pneumatic finish nailer, the other is the power miter saw.

A power miter saw will make cuts far more quickly and accurately than a circular saw or hand miter saw. It allows you to easily fine tune board lengths and angles. They don't take up much space and you can buy a decent new one for under $100. A power miter saw should be at the top of every aspiring woodworker's Christmas list.

They can be noisy and dangerous, but if you wear hearing and eye protection and use common sense you have little to fear. Just keep your hand well away from the blade while cutting and wait until the blade stops spinning before you make your next move. Also be careful when cutting little parts; the blade will sometimes fling one into the air after cutting it.

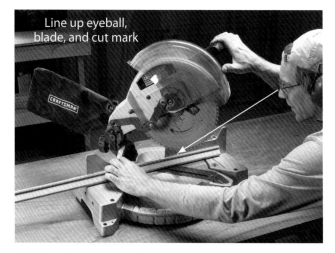

Line up eyeball, blade, and cut mark

Make Accurate Cuts

Mark your cut, position the board or molding on the miter saw table, then sight along the blade and move your work piece left or right until the edge of the blade and the mark are lined up. You'll have to retract the blade guard with your thumb in order to see, so do this without the blade spinning. Once you have the work piece accurately positioned and held firmly in place, squeeze the switch and slowly lower the blade until it's made the cut, then release the switch.

Support block

Support Your Workpiece

Always support the ends of long boards and moldings on a block of wood, or something else, that's the same height as your miter saw table. It will allow you to position the board more accurately before the cut and prevent the board from bouncing or moving after the cut.

Stop block

Make Repetitive Cuts

Clamp a stop block to your miter saw fence to make repetitive cuts. Hold onto the piece of wood that's between the block and the blade; otherwise you risk binding the blade and launching pieces of wood into the air. For longer pieces, build a temporary table out of 2x4s that extends beyond the miter saw table and secure your stop block to that.

Pedestal Picnic Table

An easy way to build a comfortable table

The picnic table we had when I was a kid was one of those "Leave it to Beaver" A-frame jobs with the attached seats you had to slither through to sit down on—and once you were seated there was always a sliver in your rear end and a brace banging you in the shin.

This one has independent benches so they're easier to sit on and it has fewer braces in awkward spots so there's less to bump your knees on. This one's more versatile, too—if you need an extra bench for the deck, patio or firepit, you've got it. Picnic tables get dragged around, rained on, and jumped off of—so don't scrimp on the screws and construction adhesive; make your table and benches as solid as possible.

We used treated wood, but cedar or redwood are also good choices.

STUFF YOU'LL NEED	
For the table:	
2" x 6" x 8'	1
2" x 4" x 8'	4
5/4" x 6" x 6'	6
For the bench:	
2" x 6" x 6'	1
2" x 4" x 8'	3
5/4" x 6" x 6'	3

Table Detail

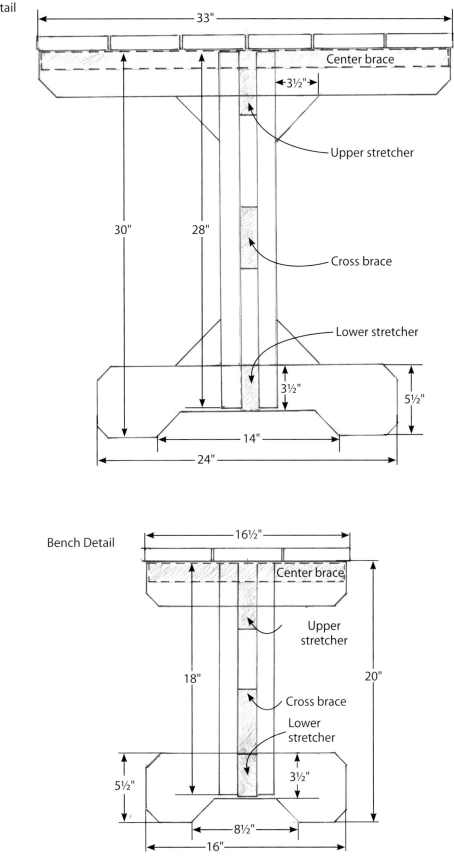

33"

Center brace

3½"

Upper stretcher

30"   28"

Cross brace

Lower stretcher

3½"

5½"

14"

24"

Bench Detail

16½"

Center brace

Upper
stretcher

18"   20"

Cross brace

Lower
stretcher

5½"   3½"

8½"

16"

How to build it

The table consists of two leg or trestle assemblies, connected by a pair of stretchers, topped off with deck boards. Begin by cutting notches in both ends of the trestle uprights (photo 1). For crisp, square-corner notches, cut as far as you can with a circular saw, then finish with a jigsaw.

Make the cutouts in the 2x6 trestle bottom member, then nestle it and the top member into the notches of the uprights (photo 2). Secure them with exterior adhesive and 3½-in. galvanized screws. Use a square to make sure the legs and horizontal members meet at right angles.

With the trestle assemblies upside down, secure the 2x4 top and bottom stretchers to them using long screws and construction adhesive (photo 3). Install the top stretcher 1½ inches below the tops of the trestles in order to accommodate the middle support strut shown in photo 5. Add the long and short cross braces

(photo 4), making sure the stretchers are square to the trestle legs.

Screw the middle support strut to the top runner and add short braces to support that. Install the top boards starting at the middle and working out (photo 5). If your wood is still wet, install the boards tight against one another; the gap should be just right by the time they dry out. Make sure the top boards overhang the trestles equally on both ends.

The benches are simply mini-versions of the table and are built the same way.

> ## TIP ★ *Add Stability*
>
> If your table is going to be subjected to lots of use and abuse, install lag screws instead of galvanized screws when building the framework.

Leg uprights

1 Mark the notches in the ends of the four leg uprights, then use a circular saw and jigsaw to cut them out.

Scrap blocks

2 Position the top and bottom members of the trestle in the notches, then secure them with outdoor construction adhesive and 3½-in. galvanized screws. Use scrap blocks to make sure the uprights are 1½ in. apart.

3 Install the top and bottom 2x4 stretchers. Position the top one 1½ in. below the tops of the trestles, and the bottom one even with the trestle base. The stretchers establish the length of your table. For a table with 6 ft. long top boards, the runners should be 63 in. long.

Bottom stretcher

Top stretcher

1½" spacer blocks

Cross brace

16"

4 Use a square to make certain the pedestals and stretchers are square to one another, then add cross braces. Install the smaller triangles (see photo 5) to brace the horizontal members of the trestle.

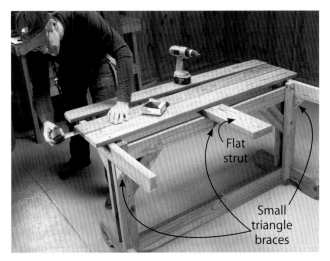

Flat strut

Small triangle braces

5 Screw the flat strut to the middle of the top stretcher to help support the top boards. Measure so the top boards overhang both ends evenly—in this case, 3 inches—then secure them with 3-in. galvanized screws.

Patio Side Table
Made 100% from 2x2s

Here's a project that requires only one type of board—the ever versatile 2x2. Most home centers stock 2x2s in their "Deck Materials" aisle, and sell them as 4-ft. long spindles or railing pickets. We made ours from clear, knot-free cedar, but lower grades of cedar and treated pine are also widely available. If you plan on using it indoors, you can use any type of wood.

How to build it

Since 2x2s vary greatly in dimension, take the time to do the layout procedure shown in photo 1. Otherwise, your blocks and slats for the tabletop won't fit evenly in the space you've created.

Use waterproof glue, like Titebond III, for all your leg, frame and slat connections. Assemble three sides of the frame (photo 2), install two legs, then squeeze them in place with the short 2x2 blocks and the first long slat. Keep adding short blocks and long slats, securing them to one another and the outer frame when possible. When you near the end, install the fourth member of the frame, then the last two legs and the last slat and blocks.

4" blocks

1 Mark out an odd number of 2x2 spaces using the short precut blocks you'll use later on as spacers. Mark the short end of the miter and cut four identical length frame members.

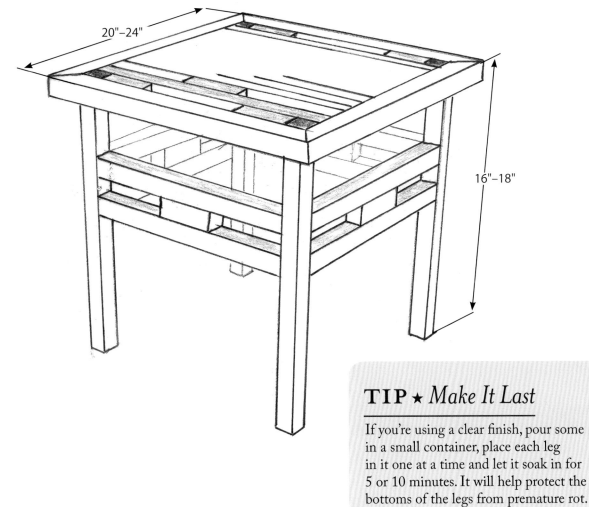

20"–24"

16"–18"

TIP ★ *Make It Last*

If you're using a clear finish, pour some in a small container, place each leg in it one at a time and let it soak in for 5 or 10 minutes. It will help protect the bottoms of the legs from premature rot.

Measure the distance between the legs close to where they meet the tabletop; the measurements should be the same on all four sides. Build the cross member assemblies (photo 3), using a square to make sure the ends are even. Use little scrap blocks (photo 4) to prop the leg assemblies at the right height, then secure them in place with 3-in. long exterior screws.

Apply at least two coats of clear finish. We had a piece of tempered glass cut to fit the tabletop. You don't have to do this—but wine glasses and other beverages will be in jeopardy of tipping if you don't.

16"–18" legs

2 Assemble three sides of the outside frame, then glue and nail a leg in each corner. Add the short and long 2x2s working toward the open side, then add the last mitered frame piece and two legs.

3 Pre-build the leg cross assemblies, making sure the ends are square to one another. Secure them with galvanized nails and waterproof glue.

Temporary spacers

4 Install the leg cross members. Use short 2x2 spacers to hold the cross members in place as you secure them with exterior screws.

Imperial to Metric Conversion

Inches	mm*	inches	mm*	inches	mm
1/64	0.40	33/64	13.10	1	25.4
1/32	0.79	17/32	13.49	2	50.8
3/64	1.19	35/64	13.89	3	76.2
1/16	1.59	9/16	14.29	4	101.6
5/64	1.98	37/64	14.68	5	127.0
3/32	2.38	19/32	15.08	6	152.4
7/64	2.78	39/64	15.48	7	177.8
1/8	3.18	5/8	15.88	8	203.2
9/64	3.57	41/64	16.27	9	228.6
5/32	3.97	21/32	16.67	10	254.0
11/64	4.37	43/64	17.07	11	279.4
3/16	4.76	11/16	17.46	12	304.8
13/64	5.16	45/64	17.86	13	330.2
7/32	5.56	23/32	18.26	14	355.6
15/64	5.95	47/64	18.65	15	381.0
1/4	6.35	3/4	19.05	16	406.4
17/64	6.75	49/64	19.45	17	431.8
9/32	7.14	25/32	19.84	18	457.2
19/64	7.54	51/64	20.24	19	482.6
5/16	7.94	13/16	20.64	20	508.0
21/64	8.33	53/64	21.03	21	533.4
11/32	8.73	27/32	21.43	22	558.8
23/64	9.13	55/64	21.83	23	584.2
3/8	9.53	7/8	22.23	24	609.6
25/64	9.92	57/64	22.62	25	635.0
13/32	10.32	29/32	23.02	26	660.4
27/64	10.72	59/64	23.42	27	685.8
7/16	11.11	15/16	23.81	28	711.2
29/64	11.51	61/64	24.21	29	736.6
15/32	11.91	31/32	24.61	30	762.0
31/64	12.30	63/64	25.00	31	787.4
1/2	12.70	1 inch	25.40	32	812.8

*Rounded to the nearest 0.01 mm

Ridiculously Simple Biographies

Spike Carlsen has been involved in the world of wood and woodworking for over 30 years. He is the former Executive Editor of *The Family Handyman* magazine, and is a regular contributor to *American Woodworker*, *FreshHome* and *Men's Health* magazines. He is the author of *A Splintered History of Wood: Belt Sander Races, Blind Woodworkers and Baseball Bats*, selected as an NPR Best Book of the Year. He lives in Stillwater, Minnesota with his wife, Kat.

Bill Zuehlke has worked behind the camera for over 30 years and shot photographs for 100s of articles and projects for *American Woodworker*, *The Family Handyman*, *Reader's Digest*, *Backyard Living* and other magazines. His work has been included in dozens of books and annuals. Other interests include reading, golf and restoring old British cars.

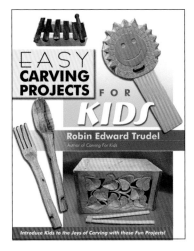

Easy Carving Projects for Kids
110 pp. $16.95
978-1-933502-30-4

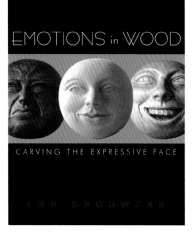

Emotions in Wood:
Carving the Expressive Face
128 pp. $19.95
978-1-933502-16-8

New Wood Puzzle Designs
96 pp. $21.95
978-0-941936-57-6

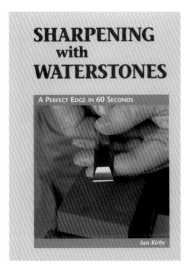

Sharpening with Waterstones:
A Perfect Edge in 60 Seconds
96 pp. $14.95
978-0-941936-76-7

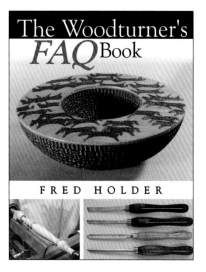

The Woodturners FAQ Book
126 pp. $19.95
978-0-941936-94-1

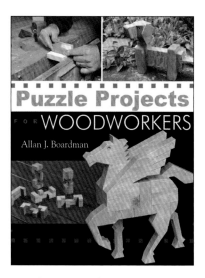

Puzzle Projects for Woodworkers
96 pp. $19.95
978-1-933502-11-3

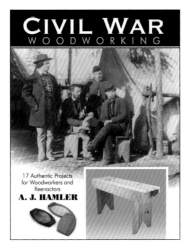

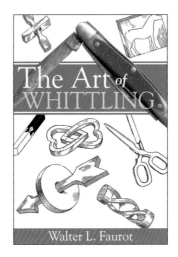

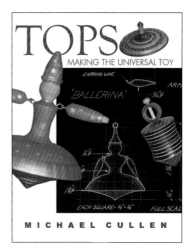

Civil War Woodworking
164 pp. $24.95
978-1-933502-28-1

The Art of Whittling
91 pp. $9.95
978-1-933502-07-6

Tops: Making the Universal Toy
128 pp. $17.95
978-1-933502-17-5

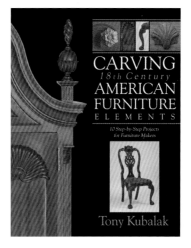

Carving for Kids
104 pp. $16.95
978-1-933502-02-1

How to Choose and Use Bench Planes
110 pp. $21.95
978-1-933502-29-8

Carving 19th Century American Furniture Elements
102 pp. $24.95
978-1-933502-32-8